"This series is a tremendous resource for the understanding of how the gospel is woven throughout Scripture. Here are gospel-minded pastors and scholars doing gospel business from all the Scriptures. This is a biblical and theological feast preparing God's people to apply the entire Bible to all of life with heart and mind wholly committed to Christ's priorities."

BRYAN CHAPELL, President Emeritus, Covenant Theological Seminary; Senior Pastor, Grace Presbyterian Church, Peoria, Illinois

"Mark Twain may have smiled when he wrote to a friend, 'I didn't have time to write you a short letter, so I wrote you a long letter.' But the truth of Twain's remark remains serious and universal, because well-reasoned, compact writing requires extra time and extra hard work. And this is what we have in the Crossway Bible study series *Knowing the Bible*. The skilled authors and notable editors provide the contours of each book of the Bible as well as the grand theological themes that bind them together as one Book. Here, in a 12-week format, are carefully wrought studies that will ignite the mind and the heart."

R. KENT HUGHES, Visiting Professor of Practical Theology, Westminster Theological Seminary

"*Knowing the Bible* brings together a gifted team of Bible teachers to produce a high-quality series of study guides. The coordinated focus of these materials is unique: biblical content, provocative questions, systematic theology, practical application, and the gospel story of God's grace presented all the way through Scripture."

PHILIP G. RYKEN, President, Wheaton College

"These *Knowing the Bible* volumes provide a significant and very welcome variation on the general run of inductive Bible studies. This series provides substantial instruction, as well as teaching through the very questions that are asked. *Knowing the Bible* then goes even further by showing how any given text links with the gospel, the whole Bible, and the formation of theology. I heartily endorse this orientation of individual books to the whole Bible and the gospel, and I applaud the demonstration that sound theology was not something invented later by Christians, but is right there in the pages of Scripture."

GRAEME L. GOLDSWORTHY, former lecturer, Moore Theological College; author, *According to Plan*, *Gospel and Kingdom*, *The Gospel in Revelation*, and *Gospel and Wisdom*

"What a gift to earnest, Bible-loving, Bible-searching believers! The organization and structure of the Bible study format presented through the *Knowing the Bible* series is so well conceived. Students of the Word are led to understand the content of passages through perceptive, guided questions, and they are given rich insights and application all along the way in the brief but illuminating sections that conclude each study. What potential growth in depth and breadth of understanding these studies offer! One can only pray that vast numbers of believers will discover more of God and the beauty of his Word through these rich studies."

BRUCE A. WARE, Professor of Christian Theology, The Southern Baptist Theological Seminary

KNOWING THE BIBLE

J. I. Packer, Theological Editor
Dane C. Ortlund, Series Editor
Lane T. Dennis, Executive Editor

•   •   •   •   •   •

Genesis	Psalms	John	1–2 Thessalonians
Exodus	Proverbs	Acts	1–2 Timothy
Leviticus	Ecclesiastes	Romans	and Titus
Deuteronomy	Isaiah	1 Corinthians	Hebrews
Joshua	Jeremiah	2 Corinthians	James
Ruth and Esther	Daniel	Galatians	1–2 Peter
1–2 Kings	Hosea	Ephesians	and Jude
Ezra and	Matthew	Philippians	Revelation
Nehemiah	Mark	Colossians and	
Job	Luke	Philemon	

•   •   •   •   •   •

J. I. PACKER is Board of Governors' Professor of Theology at Regent College (Vancouver, BC). Dr. Packer earned his DPhil at the University of Oxford. He is known and loved worldwide as the author of the best-selling book *Knowing God*, as well as many other titles on theology and the Christian life. He serves as the General Editor of the ESV Bible and as the Theological Editor for the *ESV Study Bible*.

LANE T. DENNIS is President of Crossway, a not-for-profit publishing ministry. Dr. Dennis earned his PhD from Northwestern University. He is Chair of the ESV Bible Translation Oversight Committee and Executive Editor of the *ESV Study Bible*.

DANE C. ORTLUND is Executive Vice President of Bible Publishing and Bible Publisher at Crossway. He is a graduate of Covenant Theological Seminary (MDiv, ThM) and Wheaton College (BA, PhD). Dr. Ortlund has authored several books and scholarly articles in the areas of Bible, theology, and Christian living.

1–2 THESSALONIANS

A 12-WEEK STUDY

Matt Smethurst

WHEATON, ILLINOIS

Knowing the Bible: 1–2 Thessalonians, A 12-Week Study

Copyright © 2017 by Crossway

Published by Crossway
    1300 Crescent Street
    Wheaton, Illinois 60187

Some content used in this study guide has been adapted from the *ESV Study Bible* (Crossway), copyright 2008 by Crossway, pages 2301–2320. Used by permission. All rights reserved.

Cover design: Simplicated Studio

First printing 2017

Printed in the United States of America

All emphases in Scripture quotations have been added by the author.

Trade paperback ISBN: 978-1-4335-5385-1
PDF ISBN: 978-1-4335-5386-8
Mobipocket ISBN: 978-1-4335-5387-5
EPub ISBN: 978-1-4335-5388-2

Crossway is a publishing ministry of Good News Publishers.

VP			27	26	25	24	23	22	21	20	19	18	17
15	14	13	12	11	10	9	8	7	6	5	4	3	2	1

TABLE OF CONTENTS

Series Preface: J. I. Packer and Lane T. Dennis 6

Week 1: Overview of 1 Thessalonians 7

Week 2: Thanksgiving for the Thessalonians (1 Thess. 1:1–10) 13

Week 3: Ministry to the Thessalonians (1 Thess. 2:1–16)................. 21

Week 4: Absence from the Thessalonians (1 Thess. 2:17–3:13) 29

Week 5: Holy Love Wins (1 Thess. 4:1–12)............................. 37

Week 6: The Return of the King (1 Thess. 4:13–5:11) 45

Week 7: A Parting Plea (1 Thess. 5:12–28) 53

Week 8: Overview of 2 Thessalonians 61

Week 9: The Afflicters and the Afflicted (2 Thess. 1:1–12)............... 67

Week 10: The Man of Lawlessness (2 Thess. 2:1–17) 75

Week 11: The Idle Problem (2 Thess. 3:1–18) 83

Week 12: Summary and Conclusion..................................... 91

SERIES PREFACE

KNOWING THE BIBLE, as the series title indicates, was created to help readers know and understand the meaning, the message, and the God of the Bible. Each volume in the series consists of 12 units that progressively take the reader through a clear, concise study of that book of the Bible. In this way, any given volume can fruitfully be used in a 12-week format either in group study, such as in a church-based context, or in individual study. Of course, these 12 studies could be completed in fewer or more than 12 weeks, as convenient, depending on the context in which they are used.

Each study unit gives an overview of the text at hand before digging into it with a series of questions for reflection or discussion. The unit then concludes by highlighting the gospel of grace in each passage ("Gospel Glimpses"), identifying whole-Bible themes that occur in the passage ("Whole-Bible Connections"), and pinpointing Christian doctrines that are affirmed in the passage ("Theological Soundings").

The final component to each unit is a section for reflecting on personal and practical implications from the passage at hand. The layout provides space for recording responses to the questions proposed, and we think readers need to do this to get the full benefit of the exercise. The series also includes definitions of key words. These definitions are indicated by a note number in the text and are found at the end of each chapter.

Lastly, to help understand the Bible in this deeper way, we urge readers to use the ESV Bible and the *ESV Study Bible*, which are available in various print and digital formats, including online editions at esv.org. The Knowing the Bible series is also available online. Additional 12-week studies covering each book of the Bible will be added as they become available.

May the Lord greatly bless your study as you seek to know him through knowing his Word.

J. I. Packer
Lane T. Dennis

Week 1: Overview of
1 Thessalonians

▲

Getting Acquainted

First Thessalonians covers a wide range of themes in only five short chapters: election, friendship, Satan, sex, love, work, and death, just to name a few. Yet perhaps its most dominant theme is the end times—specifically, the second coming of Jesus. As his redeemed people, Christians ought to live lives of holiness and love as we anticipate that final day. Christ's return will bring to completion all of God's promises, including judgment for his enemies and salvation for his ex-enemies—those who have become his people, his friends, and his bride. Whether now deceased (1 Thess. 4:13–18) or still living (5:1–11), anyone who has in faith embraced King Jesus is eternally secure.

Interestingly, the title "Lord Jesus" appears 11 times throughout this five-chapter letter—more than in any other New Testament epistle[1] except 2 Thessalonians (12x) and 1 Corinthians (11x). For all of Paul's emphasis on other important matters, then, the letter's ultimate focus is on the one who pervades its pages—the Lord Jesus Christ. (For further background, see the *ESV Study Bible*, pages 2301–2304; available online at www.esv.org.)

Placing 1 Thessalonians in the Larger Story

In fulfillment of God's millennia-spanning promises, Jesus the Messiah came to earth, lived, died, rose, and ascended in order to reconcile rebels to their Maker. After a dramatic conversion on the road to Damascus (Acts 9:1–19), Paul was chosen and commissioned as an apostle[2] to broadcast that gospel and to plant churches. God blessed Paul's witness in Thessalonica so much that a church was established before the apostle's abrupt exit (Acts 17:1–11). It is to this young church that he now writes from Corinth, some 360 miles (by land) to the south, addressing the Thessalonians in light of a report from Timothy's recent visit (1 Thess. 3:6). The letter's scope stretches from eternity past (1:4) to its particular focus on eternity future (1:10; 2:19–20; 3:13; 4:13–5:11, 23–24).

Key Verse

"Being affectionately desirous of you, we were ready to share with you not only the gospel of God but also our own selves, because you had become very dear to us." (1 Thess. 2:8)

Date and Historical Background

After seeing a vision of a Macedonian man urging him to "Come over to Macedonia and help us" (Acts 16:9), Paul embarked on a journey to that region with Silas and Timothy, "concluding that God had called [them] to preach the gospel" there (Acts 16:10). They traveled first to Philippi (Acts 16:11–40) before proceeding to Thessalonica.

Thessalonica was the capital of Macedonia, a Roman province in northern Greece. Boasting a population of more than 100,000, the city was a powerful commercial center in the Greco-Roman world. It was strategically located on the coast of the Aegean Sea at a key juncture along the Via Egnatia (a major Roman east-west highway). The city, therefore, attracted a diverse array of people and philosophies. This cosmopolitan makeup shaped its religious climate as well. While primarily polytheistic,[3] Thessalonica included a sizable number of monotheistic Jews.

In Acts 17:1–11, Luke recounts Paul's visit to the city. He entered the local synagogue and on three consecutive Sabbaths "reasoned with them from the Scriptures" and proclaimed Jesus as the Christ (vv. 2–3). Some of the Thessalonians "were persuaded and joined Paul and Silas, as did a great many of the devout Greeks and not a few of the leading women" (v. 4). Nevertheless, a band of jealous Jews "formed a mob, set the city in an uproar, and attacked the house of Jason, seeking to bring them out to the crowd" (v. 5). Unable to find Paul,

Silas, or Timothy, they dragged Jason and some others before the authorities and charged them with sedition: "These men who have turned the world upside down have come here also, and Jason has received them, and they are all acting against the decrees of Caesar, saying that there is another king, Jesus" (vv. 6–7). Narrowly escaping by night, Paul and his associates journeyed west to Berea, where, Luke notes, the Jews were "more noble than those in Thessalonica" (v. 11). However, on learning that Paul was in Berea, some of the Thessalonian Jews "came there too, agitating and stirring up the crowds" (v. 13). Paul again escaped, sailing south to Athens (Acts 17:16–33).

Paul's next destination was Corinth, where he remained for 18 months (Acts 18:1–18). Paul wrote to the Thessalonians from Corinth around AD 50–51, on the back end of his second missionary journey. First Thessalonians is probably his earliest New Testament letter after Galatians (c. AD 48).

Outline

I. Opening Greeting (1:1)

II. Thanksgiving and Encouragement (1:2–3:13)

    A. Thanksgiving for the Thessalonians' faith, love, and hope (1:2–3)
    B. Paul's confidence in the election of the Thessalonians (1:4–2:16)
    C. Paul's defense of the missionaries during their absence (2:17–3:10)
    D. A pastoral prayer for the Thessalonians (3:11–13)

III. Instruction and Exhortation (4:1–5:28)

    A. On pleasing God (4:1–12)
    B. On the second coming of Jesus (4:13–5:11)
    C. On community conduct (5:12–22)
    D. Prayer, assurance, and conclusion (5:23–28)

As You Get Started

Do you have a sense of any specific themes in 1 Thessalonians? Without using your Bible, do any passages from the book come to mind? Has the book been meaningful to your Christian life in any way?

If 1 Thessalonians could somehow be erased from the Scriptures and wiped from our memories, what would we lose? What do you think are some of 1 Thessalonians' crucial truths for believers?

What is your general understanding of the role of 1 Thessalonians in Scripture as a whole? What does it uniquely contribute to Christian theology? That is, how does this letter crystallize our understanding of God, salvation, the church, the end times, or any other doctrine?

What aspects of 1 Thessalonians have confused you in the past? Are there any specific questions you hope to have answered through this study?

▶ As You Finish This Unit . . .

Take a few minutes to ask God to bless you with increased understanding and a transformed heart and life as you begin this study of 1 Thessalonians.

Definitions

[1] **Epistle** – A type of letter common in NT times. Epistles typically included (1) an introduction of author and recipient; (2) greetings and expressions of thanks; (3) the body of the letter; (4) personal greetings and signature; and (5) a closing doxology or blessing. Twenty-one of the NT's 27 books are epistles, 13 of which were penned by Paul.

[2] **Apostle** – A "sent one." In the NT, the word is most commonly used as a technical term for eyewitnesses of the risen Jesus whom he personally chose and commissioned to represent him.

[3] **Polytheism** – The belief in or worship of multiple (*poly*) gods (*theism*). The Thessalonians served and revered various Greco-Roman deities, including Aphrodite, Demeter, Dionysus, and Zeus. Idolatry was rampant in the city (1 Thess. 1:9).

WEEK 2: THANKSGIVING FOR THE THESSALONIANS

1 Thessalonians 1:1–10

The Place of the Passage

Paul begins his first letter to the Thessalonians with gratitude to God for their conversion and their reputation for gospel witness. He commends this young church for embodying, amid affliction, the great triad of Christian virtues: faith, love, and hope (1 Thess. 1:3). The gospel that sounded forth *to* them (v. 5) is now sounding forth *from* them (v. 8). This passage sets the stage for the rest of the letter, using inescapable triune language: "God" is mentioned seven times, "Jesus" or "Son" or "Lord" six times, and "Spirit" twice in these 10 verses alone.

The Big Picture

First Thessalonians 1:1–10 highlights the work of the triune God in electing (v. 4), calling (v. 5), and saving (v. 10) the Thessalonian church, and also highlights the work of the church in modeling (vv. 6–7) and presenting (v. 8) the gospel to a watching world.

Reflection and Discussion

Read through the complete passage for this study, 1 Thessalonians 1:1–10. Then review the following questions concerning this introductory section to 1 Thessalonians and write your notes on them. (For further background, see the *ESV Study Bible*, pages 2305–2306; available online at www.esv.org.)

1. Greeting (1:1)

Geographically, the Thessalonian believers were located in the city of Thessalonica in northern Greece. Spiritually, however, they were "in God the Father and the Lord Jesus Christ." Why do you think Paul begins by highlighting their "spiritual address"? What does it mean to be "in God the Father and the Lord Jesus Christ"? Are you spiritually located there?

"Grace[1] to you and peace" (v. 1). With the exception of Galatians, Paul begins all of his letters this way. Why do you think "grace" always precedes "peace"? What happens if we reverse this order and begin to assume that peace with God leads to grace from God?

2. The Thessalonians' Faith and Example (1:2–10)

When you think of faith, love, and hope, what related words come to mind? In verse 3, Paul tethers this triad of virtues to some remarkably active words:

14

"work," "labor," and "steadfastness." Why do you think he does this? What implications might this have as you examine your own faith, love, and hope?

Although the doctrine of election has often sparked controversy, Paul views it not as a weapon for fighting but as a tool for encouragement. How could the Thessalonians be confident that God had elected them (vv. 4–5)? How should this logic embolden you for evangelism[2]?

Just as the Thessalonians imitated Paul and his fellow workers (v. 6), so others are now imitating the Thessalonians (vv. 7–8). Have you "become an example" (see v. 7) to anyone? What about your congregation as a whole? When people watch your church's life together, do they glimpse what it means to embrace and embody Jesus Christ?

Many Christians today in the West face increasing pressure to individualize and privatize their faith. How do verses 7–8 challenge us along these lines?

If the Thessalonians have turned from idols to the "living and true God" (v. 9), what does that say about the nature of idols? What false god most distracts you from serving the true God? How is that false god lifeless instead of "living"?

In verses 9–10, Paul connects waiting (something we often think of as passive) with serving (something we usually think of as active). How does Christian waiting differ from worldly waiting, and why is this a crucial distinction?

Also in verses 9–10, the camera pans from salvation past to salvation future. Having renounced God-substitutes for God himself (v. 9), we now await the return of God's risen Son (v. 10a), who will rescue us from God's coming wrath (v. 10b). How does the description of the Thessalonians' transformation correspond to the believer's experience of past justification,[3] present sanctification,[4] and future glorification[5]?

Read through the following three sections on *Gospel Glimpses, Whole-Bible Connections*, and *Theological Soundings*. Then take time to consider and record any *Personal Implications* these sections may have for you.

Gospel Glimpses

LOVED BY GOD. This little phrase in 1 Thessalonians 1:4 is both easy and dangerous to miss. It was God's unevoked, unbridled love that moved him—before the beginning of the world—to choose for salvation (v. 4) future rebels against his throne. Contrary to popular distortion, election is a love doctrine (see Deut. 7:7–8; 10:15; Eph. 1:4–5; 2 Thess. 2:13). Scripture discusses election not to satisfy our curiosity but to humble our pride, solidify our hope, and thrill our heart.

SAVED FROM WRATH. God's wrath is his holy and settled opposition to sin and sinners. And, unlike human wrath, God's wrath is never an overreaction. Perhaps it seems to some that an eternity of hell for only a few decades of sin is not a fair sentence. But the punishment does not exceed the crime; it fits it. Hell is an infinite sentence because it punishes an infinite crime; sin is an infinite crime because it is treason against an infinite God. You have never committed a small sin, because you have never offended a small God. Yet the stunning news of Christianity is that, through repentance and reliance on Jesus, we can be rescued from the wrath to come (1 Thess. 1:10; see also 5:9; Rom. 2:5).

Whole-Bible Connections

IDOLATRY. The Thessalonians had turned from idols to God (1:9). Throughout the Old Testament, idolatry is often associated with bowing down and sacrificing to images of foreign gods. Yet this is not the whole picture. In Ezekiel 14, we learn that the Israelites "have taken their idols into their hearts" (Ezek. 14:3). Ever since the insurrection in Eden (Genesis 3), idolatry has fundamentally been a heart issue. Thus the first of the Ten Commandments simply declares, "You shall have no other gods before me" (Ex. 20:3; see also Deut. 5:7). It is important to recognize that an idol is rarely a bad thing in and of itself; instead, it is a good thing gone bad—a good thing we have inflated into an ultimate thing. An idol, therefore, is something we will either sin to get or sin if we do not get. John Calvin famously likened the human heart to an idol factory. The New Testament makes plain that one whose life is marked by idolatry will not inherit God's kingdom (1 Cor. 6:9; Eph. 5:5). Conversion is the miracle that occurs when we forsake idols for a Savior (1 Thess. 1:9), at which point the Holy Spirit begins the lifelong process of uprooting these God-substitutes from within (Col. 3:5). Thus John closes his first letter with the charge, "Little children, keep yourselves from idols" (1 John 5:21; see also 1 Cor. 10:14).

Theological Soundings

GOSPEL. Paul turns back the clock to remind the Thessalonians of when the gospel first pierced their hearts (1 Thess. 1:5). This gospel is a message, an announcement, a breaking-news headline from heaven's pressroom. Specifically, it is the joyous news of what God has accomplished in the life, death, and resurrection of Jesus—his Son and Israel's King—to reconcile rebels forever to himself.

TRINITY. In the 10 verses of chapter 1 alone, "God" appears seven times, "Jesus" or "Son" or "Lord" six times, and "Spirit" twice. Although it can be easy to miss, the New Testament is inescapably Trinitarian. Its pages brim with the harmonious activity of Father, Son, and Spirit working together to effect redemption. Orchestrated by the Father, accomplished by the Son, and applied by the Spirit, salvation from sin is a triune achievement. Great danger lurks when we underestimate the practical implications of this doctrine—one God, eternally existing in three persons. (For more on this doctrine, see the section titled "The Trinity" in the *ESV Study Bible*, pages 2513–2515; available online at www.esv.org.)

Personal Implications

Take time to reflect on the significance of 1 Thessalonians 1:1–10 for your own life today. Consider what you have learned that might lead you to praise God, repent of sin, and trust in his gracious promises. Make notes below on personal applications for your walk with the Lord based on the (1) *Gospel Glimpses*, (2) *Whole-Bible Connections*, (3) *Theological Soundings*, and (4) this passage as a whole.

1. Gospel Glimpses

2. Whole-Bible Connections

3. Theological Soundings

4. 1 Thessalonians 1:1–10

As You Finish This Unit . . .

Take a moment now to ask for the Lord's blessing and help as you continue in this study of 1 Thessalonians. And take a moment also to look back through this unit of study and to reflect on some key lessons the Lord may be teaching you.

Definitions

[1] **Grace** – Unmerited favor, especially the free gift of salvation God gives to believers through reliance on Jesus Christ.

[2] **Evangelism** – Declaring the gospel (the *evangel*) of Jesus the King, in the power of the Spirit, and calling for response—while leaving the results to God.

[3] **Justification** – The moment God declares a Christ-trusting sinner to be in right standing before him; i.e., becoming positionally righteous.

[4] **Sanctification** – The incremental, Spirit-empowered process of being conformed to Christ's image; i.e., becoming progressively righteous.

[5] **Glorification** – The moment we see Christ's face and are fully and finally freed from sin to enjoy him forever; i.e., becoming perfectly righteous.

WEEK 3: MINISTRY TO THE THESSALONIANS

1 Thessalonians 2:1–16

▲

"You know what kind of men we proved to be among you for your sake," Paul wrote in 1:5. In chapter 2 he double-clicks on that statement, as it were, to remind the church of his conduct and ministry while among them. Amid rumors and accusations concerning his apostolic credentials, Paul pauses to clarify and defend his message, motives, and methods.

The Big Picture

In 1 Thessalonians 2:1–16 Paul defends his conduct as a minister of the gospel, drawing the Thessalonians' attention to his behavior and approach among them.

Reflection and Discussion

Read through the entire text for this study, 1 Thessalonians 2:1–16. Then interact with the following questions concerning this section of 1 Thessalonians and record your responses. (For further background, see the *ESV Study Bible*, pages 2306–2307; available online at www.esv.org.)

John Stott observes, "In [1 Thessalonians 2 and 3], more perhaps than anywhere else in his letters, [Paul] discloses his mind, expresses his emotions, and bares his soul" (*The Message of 1 and 2 Thessalonians*, 45). That is quite a statement. How do you specifically see Paul's pastoral heart on display in 2:1–16?

On the surface, it seems as if Paul's primary focus in this passage is on himself and his ministry. However, what word appears repeatedly (14 times in 16 verses)? Even while defending his genuineness as an apostle, Paul's perspective is relentlessly God-centered. What about yours? When recounting your experiences, sharing your testimony, or explaining your actions, who is the main character—the hero—of your words, and why?

How did Paul's "shameful treatment" in Philippi (see Acts 16:19–40) influence his ministry to the Thessalonians (1 Thess. 2:1–2)?

What does Paul clarify concerning his message, motives, and methods—the "what," the "why," and the "how"—in the first several verses of chapter 2?

What metaphors does Paul use in this passage to describe his conduct among the Thessalonians? What is the significance of each?

Verse 8 is a beautiful statement on the importance of loving those to whom we witness. Paul points out that his ministry in Thessalonica was not a hit-and-run gospel invasion. Instead, he and his associates were happy to stay, form friendships, and invest in their new friends' lives. What are the benefits of so-called "relational" or "friendship" evangelism? Are there any dangers?

What does it mean to walk in a manner "worthy" of God (v. 12; see also 2 Thess. 1:5, 11; Eph. 4:1; Phil. 1:27; Col. 1:10)? How does such language fit the reality of God's one-way grace, which assures us that we do not earn right standing with him by living a good life?

Do you think of the gospel as something mainly for Christians or mainly for non-Christians? In 1 Thessalonians 2:13, Paul says that the "word of God"—in context synonymous with the "gospel of God" (vv. 2, 8, 9)—is "at work in you believers." In what sense is the good news active in the hearts and lives of Christians?

Suffering for the gospel was the calling not just of the apostles (1 Thess. 2:1–2) but also of the whole congregation (vv. 14–15). And the Thessalonians' opponents were not enemies from foreign lands but were their "own countrymen" (v. 14). Have you ever suffered—relationally or socially, perhaps even physically—for your Christian faith? Read and ponder Matthew 10:34–39 and Mark 10:28–30. How should Jesus' words in these passages shape our outlook on life?

How were the Jews "[opposing] all mankind" (1 Thess. 2:15)? Why do you think Paul equated opposition to evangelism (v. 16) with opposition to humanity (v. 15)? What implications might this have for our own lives?

Read through the following three sections on *Gospel Glimpses, Whole-Bible Connections,* and *Theological Soundings.* Then take time to consider and record any *Personal Implications* these sections may have for you.

Gospel Glimpses

SALVATION. In verse 16 Paul connects the work of evangelism ("speaking to the Gentiles") to the miracle of salvation ("that they might be saved"). Although we tend to speak of salvation as an exclusively past event, it is actually a past (Eph. 2:8), present (1 Cor. 15:2), and future (Rom. 5:9) reality. Salvation is the all-encompassing category for what God has achieved through Christ in order to reconcile rebels to himself. All believers in Jesus have been saved from the penalty of sin (justification), are being saved from the power of sin (sanctification), and one day will be saved from the presence of sin (glorification).

Whole-Bible Connections

ISRAEL JUDGED LIKE GENTILES. In verse 16, Paul says that the Jews who killed Jesus and who clamor to thwart gospel advance are "[filling] up the measure of their sins." This is a significant statement, as it repeats language that Genesis 15:16 applies to Gentiles.[1] As Jesus explains in the parable of the tenants (Matt. 21:33–46), national Israel forfeited their inheritance and, through serial idolatry and adultery against their covenant[2] Lord, became like the Gentiles they despised. Any Jewish person who refuses to embrace Jesus the Messiah is a covenant outsider.

Theological Soundings

STEWARDSHIP. Scripture teaches that God owns all things because he created all things. As divine image-bearers,[3] all humans have been tasked with reflecting God by ruling and cultivating the world for him. But Christians have been handed a more weighty stewardship still: the good news of King Jesus. As Paul puts it in 1 Thessalonians 2:4, "We have been approved by God to be entrusted with the gospel." *Entrusted.* This gospel treasure is not ours. It did not originate with us. It is not a rough draft. It needs no editors. Our responsibility is simply to believe it, cherish it, apply it, guard it, and proclaim it. And Paul insists that this gospel stewardship must be accompanied by pure motives and open methods: "Our appeal does not spring from error or impurity or any attempt to deceive, but just as we have been approved by God to be entrusted with the gospel, so we speak, not to please man, but to please God who tests our hearts" (1 Thess. 2:3–4).

Personal Implications

Take time to reflect on applications of 1 Thessalonians 2:1–16 for your own life today. Consider what you have learned that might lead you to praise God, repent of sin, and trust in his gracious promises. Make notes below on the personal implications for your walk with the Lord based on the (1) *Gospel Glimpses*, (2) *Whole-Bible Connections*, (3) *Theological Soundings*, and (4) this passage as a whole.

1. Gospel Glimpses

2. Whole-Bible Connections

3. Theological Soundings

4. 1 Thessalonians 2:1–16

> ## As You Finish This Unit . . .

Take a moment now to ask for the Lord's blessing and help as you continue in this study of 1 Thessalonians. And take a moment also to look back through this unit of study and reflect on key ideas the Lord may be teaching you.

Definitions

[1] **Gentiles** – The non-Jewish peoples of the world.

[2] **Covenant** – The plotline of Scripture centers on the establishment of successive covenants—God-initiated, promise-based, binding agreements between God and humans. If the Bible is the unfolding narrative of the establishment of God's kingdom, covenants are its backbone. Though there is debate over the exact number of major covenants in Scripture, many recognize covenants mediated through Adam (Genesis 1–2), Noah (Genesis 9), Abraham (Genesis 12), Moses (Exodus 19–20), David (2 Samuel 7), and a new covenant (Jeremiah 31) mediated through Christ (Luke 22:20; Hebrews 8–10). Israel was chosen out of the world to be God's covenant people: "I will walk among you and will be your God, and you shall be my people" (Lev. 26:12). From a human perspective, the OT is a long story of covenant failure—every covenant mediator and the entire nation of Israel ultimately failed to be faithful to the covenant Lord. The glory of the gospel, however, is that in Jesus Christ the covenant maker became the covenant keeper and then died for covenant breakers.

[3] **Image-bearer** – The Bible's opening pages ring with the truth that God created humans "in his image" to know and reflect him on earth (Gen. 1:26–27). Just as kings in ancient times would set up statues or "images" on the highest peaks to display their fame and rule, we too are designed to draw attention to our Maker. Though God's image in man was fractured at the fall (Genesis 3), it has not been eradicated. Jesus is the full image of the invisible God (2 Cor. 4:4; Col. 1:15; Heb. 1:3), and in Christians this image is being restored (Rom. 8:29; Eph. 4:24; Col. 3:10).

Week 4: Absence from the Thessalonians

1 Thessalonians 2:17–3:13

The Place of the Passage

Having defended his ministry among the Thessalonians in 2:1–16, Paul now defends his absence from them.

The Big Picture

Paul explains his absence, expresses concern for the Thessalonians' suffering, reaffirms his affection, and thanks God for Timothy's encouraging report.

Reflection and Discussion

Read through the passage for this study, 1 Thessalonians 2:17–3:13. Then review the following questions concerning this section of 1 Thessalonians and record your responses below. (For further background, see the *ESV Study Bible*, pages 2307–2308; available online at www.esv.org.)

1. Paul's Pastoral Heart (2:17–3:5)

Paul explains that he and his associates longed to reunite with the Thessalonians, but "Satan[1] hindered us" (2:18). What are some dangers of being under-aware of the demonic realm? What about being over-aware? From this passage, we see that Satan can hinder our plans (2:18) and tempt our hearts (3:5), but what does Paul's prayer in 3:11 assume about the scope of Satan's power?

In 2:19–20 Paul calls the Thessalonian church his "hope," his "joy," his "crown," and his "glory." This is remarkable, especially in light of all of this congregation's faults. How do you view your own local church[2]? Are you aware mainly of its faults or of its beauty? What might need to change, whether in your thoughts, speech, or behavior, to more closely resemble Paul's perspective and heart?

Paul describes Timothy not merely as *his* coworker but also as *God's* coworker (3:2). Why do you think he ascribes such a lofty and unusual title to Timothy? How does Paul's explanation in 1 Corinthians 3:5–9 clarify the meaning and significance of this title?

What are all Christians "destined" for, according to 1 Thessalonians 3:3–4? Does this surprise you? Why or why not? Notice also that Paul did not merely mention this in passing while in Thessalonica; he "kept telling" them (v. 4). This was Discipleship 101 (see also Acts 14:21–22).

2. Timothy's Encouraging News (3:6–13)

Why, according to 3:1–5, did Paul send Timothy to Thessalonica?

Having been reassured through Timothy's report, Paul declares, "Now we live, if you are standing fast in the Lord" (3:8). What are you most tempted to "stand fast in" besides the Lord? Why?

Paul's well-being is deeply bound up with the Thessalonians' well-being: their flourishing brings him comfort (v. 7), gratitude (v. 9), joy (v. 9), even life (v. 8). What are some ways to cultivate a heart that is more easily edified—even electrified—by reports of God's grace?

What can we learn about prayer—what it is, what it is for, and how to do it—from 3:11–13?

Verses 11–13 form a transitional prayer linking the previous section (2:1–3:10) to the second half of the letter (4:1–5:22). Verse 11 looks back, whereas verses 12–13 look ahead. Based on verses 12–13, what themes will feature prominently in the rest of the letter?

Read through the following three sections on *Gospel Glimpses*, *Whole-Bible Connections*, and *Theological Soundings*. Then take time to consider the *Personal Implications* these sections may have for you.

Gospel Glimpses

FREED FROM SATAN. Satan can powerfully influence you as a Christian, tempting your mind (1 Thess. 3:5) and hindering your ministry (2:18). But he no longer has mastery over you; those days are over (Eph. 2:1–2). "The reason the Son of God appeared was to destroy the works of the devil" (1 John 3:8). Take heart, then, if you are a follower of Jesus. Satan was defeated (Col. 2:13–15), Satan is being defeated (Eph. 6:10–20), and Satan will be defeated (Rom. 16:20). Yes, he "prowls around like a roaring lion, seeking someone to devour" (1 Pet. 5:8), but at Jesus' death he was defanged, and at Jesus' return he will be destroyed. No wonder Martin Luther declared in his hymn, "A Mighty Fortress Is Our God" (c. 1529), "The Prince of Darkness grim, we tremble not for him / His rage we can endure, for lo, his doom is sure / One little word shall fell him."

Whole-Bible Connections

FACE-TO-FACE COMMUNITY. Paul twice conveys his profound longing to see the Thessalonians "face to face" (2:17; 3:10). His affection for the congregation runs so deep that he describes his abrupt departure as being "torn away"—literally "orphaned" (2:17; see also Acts 17:5–11). Yet Paul's longing to reunite with the Thessalonians is not merely a striking example of Christian affection; it is also an echo of Eden and a preview of the new Eden (Genesis 1–2; Revelation 21–22). In other words, he craves face-to-face fellowship not simply because he is a Christian but also because he is *human*. Created in the image of a relational God—the Trinity, after all, is a community—we were custom-designed for unhindered union with our Maker and our neighbor alike. Ever since humanity's rebellion in Genesis 3, however, sin has infected and fractured our relationships in every direction. Still, we remain relational creatures who long to know and be known, to love and be loved. This is why there is nothing more painful—more *unnatural* on our most primal level—than the relational and physical severing of death. Yet Christianity insists that even the parting brought on by death is not the end of the story for those united to Jesus. The day is coming when the "age of the ear" will give way to the "age of the eye" (see 2 Cor. 5:7) and we will see God's face (Rev. 22:4; see also 1 Cor. 13:12; 1 John 3:2).

Theological Soundings

DIVINE SOVEREIGNTY. "Now may our God and Father himself, and our Lord Jesus, direct our way to you" (1 Thess. 3:11). Paul's prayer for divine intervention is grounded in his conviction concerning divine sovereignty. Despite Satan's hindering activity (2:18), he was not finally decisive in Paul's plans; God was. "Direct our way to you" (3:11) is not a plea for general guidance but a specific request for God to remove the demonic obstacles mentioned in 2:18. It is vital to understand and believe that Satan's havoc extends only as far as God's hand allows. One of the most comforting lessons of the book of Job, for example, is that Satan is on a leash. And though in a fallen world this leash can feel painfully long, there is an infinitely wise hand at the end of it. He who is for you in Christ (Rom. 8:31), who refused to spare even his own Son for you (Rom. 8:32), will thwart your enemy's ultimate goals, bending them instead for your ultimate good (Rom. 8:28).

▶ Personal Implications

Take time to reflect on the implications of 1 Thessalonians 2:17–3:13 for your own life today. Consider what you have learned that might lead you to praise God, repent of sin, and trust in his gracious promises. Make notes below on personal applications for your walk with the Lord based on the (1) *Gospel Glimpses*, (2) *Whole-Bible Connections*, (3) *Theological Soundings*, and (4) this passage as a whole.

1. Gospel Glimpses

2. Whole-Bible Connections

3. Theological Soundings

4. 1 Thessalonians 2:17–3:13

> ## As You Finish This Unit . . .

Take a moment now to ask for the Lord's blessing and help as you continue in this study of 1 Thessalonians. And take a moment also to look back through this unit of study, to reflect on some key lessons the Lord may be teaching you.

Definitions

[1] **Satan** – A personal supernatural being who is the great deceiver (Rev. 12:9), the captain of demonic forces (Matt. 12:24), and the archenemy of God and his people. Satan was the first sinner; indeed, he has "been sinning from the beginning" (1 John 3:8). Jesus called him the "father of lies" and "a murderer from the beginning" (John 8:44)—language harking back to the dawn of history. Elsewhere he is called "the evil one" (Matt. 13:19), "the ruler of this world" (John 12:31), "the god of this world" (2 Cor. 4:4), and "the prince of the power of the air" (Eph. 2:2). In Scripture we witness Satan spearheading attacks on God's people (Job 1:6; 1 Chron. 21:1; Zech. 3:1), with "power" (Acts 26:18) to bind (Luke 13:16) and "oppress" (Acts 10:38). Nevertheless, he is no match for heaven's King. The Devil was defeated (Col. 2:13–15), is being defeated (Eph. 6:10–20), and will be defeated (Rom. 16:20; Rev. 20:10).

[2] **Local church** – A covenant body of believers who assemble under the right preaching of the Word and the right administration of the sacraments, or ordinances (baptism and the Lord's Supper). Put another way, a church is an embassy of heaven on Planet Earth, a covenant body of baptized Christians who regularly gather for worship and scatter for witness—although the worship is also witness and the witness is also worship. The Christian life is a churched life; believers are knit together as children in God's family (1 Tim. 3:15), members of Christ's body (1 Cor. 12:12–14), and stones in the Spirit's temple (1 Cor. 3:16; Eph. 2:20). Membership in the universal church finds expression in formal commitment to a local church.

WEEK 5: HOLY LOVE WINS

1 Thessalonians 4:1–12

The Place of the Passage

Paul has commended the Thessalonians for their faith and witness (1 Thess. 1:2–10), defended his own conduct and ministry (2:1–16), explained his absence (2:17–3:5), and rejoiced in Timothy's report (3:6–13). He now turns to consider a few specific pastoral issues, beginning with holiness (4:1–8), love (4:9–10), and work (4:11–12).

The Big Picture

In 1 Thessalonians 4:1–12 we see that a God-pleasing life has both moral and social dimensions, characterized by holiness and love.

Reflection and Discussion

Read through the complete passage for this study, 1 Thessalonians 4:1–12. Then review the questions below concerning this section of 1 Thessalonians and record your responses below. (For further background, see the *ESV Study Bible*, pages 2308–2309; available online at www.esv.org.)

What is the relationship between Paul's prayer in 3:12–13 and his instructions in 4:1–12?

Take a moment to ponder what it means to "please God" (v. 1; see also 2:4). What does this simple yet profound truth—that we can bring pleasure to our Maker's heart—imply about who he is and what he is like?

Have you ever wanted to know the will of God for your life? Thankfully, this passage offers a definitive answer. What is God's expressed will for you, according to verse 3?

We find ourselves amid a sexualized culture, even a sexual revolution, in the West. Words like "abstain" (v. 3) and "control" (v. 4) in reference to sexual expression sound prudish, even intolerant, to many. But in what ways does our culture misunderstand the Bible's sexual ethic? How is God's design for sexuality both counterculturally beautiful and counterintuitively freeing?

If Paul were writing to the church today, what do you think he would say regarding sexuality?

According to verse 5, the "passion of lust" marks those who "do not know God." In what ways does giving in to lust constitute—or reveal—functional atheism[1]?

Which persons of the Trinity make an appearance in 4:1–8, and why is this significant? Why do you think the Holy Spirit in particular is mentioned in verse 8?

According to Paul, one reason we should work faithfully is so that we may "walk properly before outsiders" (v. 12). Indeed, to be "well thought of by outsiders" is a qualification for church elders[2] (1 Tim. 3:7). Nevertheless, did not Jesus say, "Woe to you, when all people speak well of you" (Luke 6:26), and "You will be hated by all for my name's sake" (Luke 21:17)? How do we reconcile such texts?

How do you think unbelieving "outsiders" view your local church, and why? How do you think "outsiders" in your own life—whether family or friends or neighbors or coworkers—view you, and why?

Read through the following three sections on *Gospel Glimpses*, *Whole-Bible Connections*, and *Theological Soundings*. Then take time to consider the *Personal Implications* these sections may have for you.

▶ Gospel Glimpses

HOLINESS. The specific focus of 1 Thessalonians 4:1–8 is Christian holiness, not Christ's holiness. The growing presence of holiness in our lives is a necessary and indispensable fruit of grace—without which we will not see the Lord (Heb. 12:14). Nevertheless, we can scarcely read this passage without becoming freshly aware of our need for a perfectly holy Redeemer—and freshly thankful that we have one in Christ. Who among us has walked rightly and pleased God without fail (1 Thess. 4:1)? Who among us has abstained from sexual immorality not only in action but also in thought (v. 3)? Who among us has not

40

fallen into various forms of impurity (v. 7)? Praise God, then, for the one who is gloriously unlike us. "It was indeed fitting," the author of Hebrews observes, "that we should have such a high priest, holy, innocent, unstained, separated from sinners, and exalted above the heavens" (Heb. 7:26). A Christian is someone who reads 1 Thessalonians 4:1–8 and finds a fountain of exhortation but not a drop of condemnation (Rom. 8:1). The moral spotlessness of Jesus—freely imputed through faith to moral wrecks like us—is the foundation of a Spirit-empowered, grace-fueled life.

KNOWING GOD. First Thessalonians 4:5 speaks of Gentiles who "do not know God." What does it mean to know God? Surely it entails more than merely knowing *about* him. The Devil knows more about God than you do, but he hates what he knows. Biblically, knowing God refers to a vital, personal, intimate union—more like spouse knowledge than stranger knowledge. Indeed, knowing God through Christ is the essence of eternal life. "This is eternal life," Jesus explains, "that they know you the only true God, and Jesus Christ whom you have sent" (John 17:3). In the final analysis, what matters most is not whether you claim to know God, but whether God knows you. As Paul makes clear to the Galatians, "You have come to know God, or rather to be known by God" (Gal. 4:9). Most famously, Jesus concludes the Sermon on the Mount with a warning that on the last day many will claim to have been ministry superstars in his name, to which he will respond with terrifying words: "I never knew you; depart from me, you workers of lawlessness" (Matt. 7:23). In other words, many brandishing mighty ministry résumés will hear, "I knew all *that*, but I never knew *you*."

▶ Whole-Bible Connections

SEXUAL IMMORALITY. As the Bible's storyline unfolds, a number of social issues seem to develop in a more "progressive" direction. In the New Testament, for example, both women and ethnic minorities are elevated and liberated in countercultural ways (see Gal. 3:28; Col. 3:11; 1 Pet. 3:7; Eph. 2:11–22; Philem. 1–25). Yet there is one significant exception to this overall "progressive" trend: sexual ethics. If anything, in fact, Scripture's sexual ethics develop in a more *conservative* direction as we enter the New Testament. In the Old Testament polygamy was permitted, for example, though never condoned. Likewise, Old Testament concessions for divorce had been abused into licenses to leave one's wife "for any cause" (Matt. 19:3). Once we get to the Gospels, however, Jesus is strikingly restrictive on sexual matters. As Jesus and the apostles liberate slaves and women by undermining the institution of slavery and cultural habits of chauvinism, not once do they "liberate" anyone sexually. Even the adulterous woman in John 8 (the story's questioned authenticity notwithstanding) is told to "go, and from now on sin no more"

(v. 11). Whether the issue is polygamy or divorce or fornication or adultery or homosexuality, the New Testament tightens the standards by summoning us back to God's good creation design. Paul's language in 1 Thessalonians 4 to "abstain from sexual immorality" (v. 3) and to "control [your] own body in holiness and honor" (v. 4), then, is neither prudish nor at odds with Jesus' teaching; it is par for the course in the New Testament.

Theological Soundings

PURITY OF THE CHURCH. Paul's entire discussion in 1 Thessalonians 4:1–8 presupposes that corporate holiness is not optional. Earlier he appealed to his own example of holiness (2:10) and prayed for the church to be marked by the same (3:13). God's people have always been expected to be holy—morally set apart from the world and consecrated to him—for only a distinct people can reflect the character of a distinct God (Lev. 20:26; Matt. 5:14–16, 48; Phil. 2:14–15; 1 Pet. 1:14–16; 2:9–10; 2 Tim. 2:20–22). The Bible's charge to holiness is a summons not to withdraw from the world but to point to a better way. It is about consecration, not retreat; separation, not seclusion (John 17:15; 1 Cor. 5:9–13; 1 Pet. 2:11–12). Those who bear God's name must reflect his character. To be sure, the church is not a gathering of the perfect—far from it. But it *is* a gathering of the repentant. In fact, the only thing that warrants formal exclusion from church membership is unrepentance (Matt. 18:15–20; 1 Cor. 5:1–13). Church discipline is simply telling an unrepentant church member, "Because your life no longer honors Christ, we can no longer affirm you as a believer." Pursuing gospel-grounded, grace-fueled holiness in our churches is an essential part of our obedience, our witness, and our joy.

HOLY SPIRIT. Who is the "Holy Spirit" that God gives to Christians (1 Thess. 4:8)? He is the eternal third person of the Trinity who appears throughout Scripture, from the first page (Gen. 1:2) to the last (Rev. 22:17). The Holy Spirit is not a force but a fully divine person. In Acts 5 Peter tells Ananias, "Why has Satan filled your heart to lie to *the Holy Spirit?*" (v. 3). The next verse reads, "You have not lied to man but to *God*" (v. 4). As God, the Spirit is our omnipotent Helper (John 15:26) whose role within the Trinity includes bearing witness to Jesus (John 15:26), producing fruit in believers (Gal. 5:22–23), and giving gifts to the church (1 Cor. 12:1–11).

Personal Implications

Take time to reflect on the implications of 1 Thessalonians 4:1–12 for your own life today. Consider what you have learned that might lead you to praise God, repent of sin, and trust in his gracious promises. Make notes below on the personal applications for your walk with the Lord based on the (1) *Gospel Glimpses*, (2) *Whole-Bible Connections*, (3) *Theological Soundings*, and (4) this passage as a whole.

1. Gospel Glimpses

2. Whole-Bible Connections

3. Theological Soundings

4. 1 Thessalonians 4:1–12

As You Finish This Unit . . .

Take a moment now to ask for the Lord's blessing and help as you continue in this study of 1 Thessalonians. And take a moment also to look back through this unit of study and to reflect on some key lessons the Lord may be teaching you.

Definitions

[1] **Functional atheism** – Living as if God does not exist.

[2] **Elder** – A formally recognized leader in a local church with authority to teach, guard, and shepherd Christ's flock. Qualifications for elders are listed in 1 Timothy 3:1–7 and Titus 1:5–9. The NT uses the terms "elder" (*presbyteros*), "overseer/bishop" (*episkopos*), and "pastor" (*poimēn*) interchangeably, each referring to the same office (see, for example, Acts 20:17–28; 1 Pet. 5:1–5; Titus 1:5–7). Moreover, the overwhelming NT pattern is that a church ought to be led by a plurality of elders, not by a lone pastor. This example of plural-elder leadership is confirmed by Luke (Acts 11:30; 14:23; 15:2, 4, 6, 22–23, 16:4; 20:17; 21:18); Paul (1 Tim. 4:14; 5:17; Titus 1:5); James (James 5:14); Peter (1 Pet. 5:1, 5); and the author of Hebrews (Heb. 13:7, 17).

Week 6: The Return of the King

1 Thessalonians 4:13–5:11

The Place of the Passage

Having addressed the subjects of holiness (1 Thess. 4:1–8) and, more briefly, love (4:9–10) and work (4:11–12), Paul now discusses how our future should shape our present—that is, how our hope should affect our life.

The Big Picture

In 1 Thessalonians 4:13–5:11 Paul fast-forwards to the future to discuss the return of Jesus (4:13–18) and the day of the Lord (5:1–11)—and how Christians are to live in light of this breathtaking hope.

> ### Reflection and Discussion

Read through 1 Thessalonians 4:13–5:11, the focus of this week's study. Following this, review the questions below concerning this section of 1 Thessalonians and record your responses. (For further background, see the *ESV Study Bible*, pages 2309–2310; available online at www.esv.org.)

1. The Return of the Lord (4:13–18)

Since Christians have such a stunning hope, does Paul expect us not to grieve (v. 13)? Why or why not? How should our hope affect the way in which we grieve?

Summarize the sequence of events in these verses. Does the language of verse 16 suggest that Christ's return will be a secret event (recognized only by Christians) or a public event (recognized by all)?

According to verse 16, deceased Christians will be raised in response to Christ's "cry of command." It is a bit odd to think of dead persons being commanded to do something they themselves cannot do. But what is the theological significance of this? For example, in what ways does this verse correspond to the story of Lazarus in John 11? How about Ephesians 2:1–10?

As you read Paul's description of your future in verses 13–18, which words capture your heart most? Amid the clamor of archangels and trumpets and dead bodies being infused with life, do not overlook the end of verse 17. Why is this the most wonderful promise of the entire passage?

2. The Day of the Lord (5:1–11)

What is the relationship between the event in 4:13–18 and the event in 5:1–11? Is Paul describing two comings or one?

Read Matthew 24:36–51 and note from where Paul draws his language of the day of the Lord as being like a "thief in the night" (1 Thess. 5:2). Will the day come as a sudden surprise for believers? Why or why not?

The day of the Lord will be sudden (v. 3) and surprising (v. 4) to those in darkness, preceded by confident declarations such as, "There is peace and security" (v. 3). Although the immediate cultural backdrop of Paul's words was likely Roman imperial propaganda declaring the *pax romana*—the peace of Rome— the sentiment is still relevant today. Where in our current culture do you see the assumption that there is peace and security? Where are you most tempted to find peace and security outside of Jesus?

Beginning in verse 4, Paul develops a contrast between children of the day (or light) and children of the night (or darkness). Every human being is in one group or the other; there is no third option. What beliefs and behaviors characterize each category? Which one best describes you?

Explain how verse 8 harks back to 1:3. Additionally, how should passages describing the "equipment" worn by the Messiah (e.g., Isa. 59:17; see also 11:5; 52:7) illumine our understanding of how Christians are equipped? Describe how verse 8 is similar to Paul's description of the believer's battle attire in Ephesians 6:10–20? What differences do you notice?

First Thessalonians 5:9 tells us what believers are *not* "destined" for. Where else in 1 Thessalonians have we encountered this word? How should we understand the relationship between the promises in these two passages—and how should we live in light of them?

In what ways are eschatology[1] and ethics "twin siblings," according to 1 Thessalonians 4:13–5:11?

Read through the following three sections on *Gospel Glimpses, Whole-Bible Connections,* and *Theological Soundings*. Then take time to consider the *Personal Implications* these sections may have for you.

Gospel Glimpses

DESTINED FOR SALVATION. In 1 Thessalonians 5:9–10, we encounter gospel treasure shrink-wrapped in one sentence (see also 4:14). Paul presents divine salvation as the divine alternative to divine wrath. We are rescued *from* God *by* God—from his justice, by his mercy. And this is not accidental; this was not "Plan B." Before the beginning, the triune God "destined" a specific people for a specific end: salvation. If you are a repenting[2] believer in Jesus, judgment will not have the last word in your life. It is not your destiny. God destined his Son for wrath instead of you. On the cross, Jesus was treated as if he had lived *your* (sinful) life so that, through faith in him, you could be treated as if you have lived *his* (sinless) life.

SUBSTITUTE AND FRIEND. In verse 10, Paul declares that Jesus died *for* us so that we might live *with* him. Consider the order of those two prepositions and the relationship between them. What would happen if they were reversed? The declaration would become, "Jesus died *with* us that we might live *for* him." Why would that be bad news? Here is why: If Jesus had only died *with* us (as our example), we might have been enabled to live *for* him (as his servant), but that would have been all. But because he also died *for* us (as our substitute), we can also live *with* him (as his friend). Praise God for the gospel!

Whole-Bible Connections

LIGHT AND DARKNESS. From God's light-creating word in Genesis 1:3 to his light-engulfing glory in Revelation 22:5, the theme of light and darkness pervades Scripture. Whereas light often represents God's holiness (1 John 1:5) or guidance (Pss. 43:3; 119:105), darkness often signifies human rebellion (John 3:19) or confusion (Prov. 4:19). Indeed, God's own character is marked by moral purity—light without any trace of darkness (1 John 1:5; see also Pss. 27:1; 104:2; Dan. 2:22; 1 Tim. 6:16). Most significantly, Jesus himself is the light of the world (John 1:4–9; 8:12), and his redeemed people—those who have been transferred from darkness to light (Col. 1:13; 1 Pet. 2:9) by seeing the light of his glory[3] streaming through the gospel (2 Cor. 4:4, 6)—are called to live as shining witnesses in a dark and hostile world (Matt. 5:14–16; John 12:36; Phil. 2:14–16). The children of light (Eph. 5:8; 1 Thess. 5:5) must dress themselves daily in the armor of light (Rom. 13:12).

DEATH AS SLEEP. Because of the certainty of our resurrection hope, the New Testament often likens Christian death to a long nap. Such "sleep" is temporary, for Jesus will soon return to raise the dead. Paul uses sleep language no less than four times in this passage (4:13, 14, 15; 5:10) to underscore the impermanence of death and the certainty of resurrection life. And this way of speaking is not anomalous; we encounter the same hope-filled assurance on the lips of Jesus (John 11:11–13) and in the words of Matthew (Matt. 27:52); Luke (Acts 7:60; 13:36); Peter (2 Pet. 3:4); and, again, Paul (1 Cor. 15:6, 18, 20).

▶ Theological Soundings

THE RETURN OF CHRIST. One day, heaven's risen and reigning King will return—suddenly, physically, triumphantly—to the earth he made. He will extend justice to his enemies and mercy to his ex-enemies. All things will be made new. So Christians have always hoped and believed. But here the consensus screeches to a halt. Will Jesus secretly snatch away his church seven years prior to his climactic return? Will his return launch a thousand-year earthly rule before the final judgment and eternal state? Or is the so-called millennium happening now via his heavenly reign? These and other questions concerning the timing and sequence of events associated with Christ's return abound. Some who espouse a "pretribulational rapture" believe that he will return twice—first in secret for his church and again seven years later publicly to inaugurate his millennial reign. Putting 1 Thessalonians 4:13–18 alongside 5:1–11, however, this theory becomes difficult to sustain, for it appears that the return of the Lord (described in 4:13–18) and the day of the Lord (described in 5:1–11) are the same event. This becomes even more clear at the outset of 2 Thessalonians, where the coming of Christ to save believers and to punish unbelievers is a single, simultaneous event. In fact, in contrast to the notion that Christ's return to save precedes his return to judge by a period of seven years, in 2 Thessalonians his punitive action is mentioned first (see 2 Thess. 1:6–7).

SOBER-MINDEDNESS. Twice in this passage Paul summons Christians to be sober, for we belong to the day rather than to the night (1 Thess. 5:6, 8). What does this mean? Throughout the New Testament, moral and spiritual sobriety—clear-headedness—is held forth as an indispensable virtue for believers (Rom. 12:3; 2 Tim. 4:5; Titus 2:2; 1 Pet. 1:13; 4:7; 5:8) and a basic qualification for elders (1 Tim. 3:2) and deacons (1 Tim. 3:8, compare v. 11). Such sobriety is often associated with a posture of alertness—of watchfulness—since the enemy is fierce (1 Pet. 5:8) and the end is near (1 Pet. 4:7; see also 1 Thess. 5:6–8). Rather than being drunk with worldly wisdom or substances such as wine, then, we are to be filled with the Holy Spirit (Eph. 5:18), controlled and led by him (Rom. 8:14; Gal. 5:18).

Personal Implications

Take time to reflect on the implications of 1 Thessalonians 4:13–5:11 for your own life today. Consider what you have learned that might lead you to praise God, repent of sin, and trust in his gracious promises. Make notes below on the personal implications for your walk with the Lord based on the (1) *Gospel Glimpses*, (2) *Whole-Bible Connections*, (3) *Theological Soundings*, and (4) this passage as a whole.

1. Gospel Glimpses

2. Whole-Bible Connections

3. Theological Soundings

4. 1 Thessalonians 4:13–5:11

> ### As You Finish This Unit . . .

Take a moment now to ask for the Lord's blessing and help as you continue in this study of 1 Thessalonians. And take a moment also to look back through this unit of study and reflect on some key lessons the Lord may be teaching you.

Definitions

[1] **Eschatology** – The study of "last things," typically referring to the events surrounding Jesus' return at the end of time.

[2] **Repentance** – A complete change of heart and mind resulting in one's turning from sin to faith in Jesus. Without it—without renouncing our sin and relying on Christ—there is no salvation. Repentance is both a command (Acts 3:19) and a gift (John 6:65; Acts 3:26; 5:31; 11:18; 2 Tim. 2:25), indispensable to spiritual flourishing. It both starts (justification) and marks (sanctification) the Christian life. Indeed, repentance is one of the main vehicles linking us to our Savior on a daily, even hourly, basis. True regeneration and conversion is always accompanied by repentance.

[3] **Glory** – The beauty of God gone public. The Scriptures are saturated with the theme of God's glory—a glory that shines brightest in the person and work of Jesus. The Bible testifies to the glory of God in eternity past (John 17:1, 4–5), in creation (Ps. 19:1; Isa. 43:6–7, 21; Col. 1:16–18), in redemption (Ps. 79:9; Jer. 14:7, 21; Rom. 3:23–26; 2 Cor. 4:4), and in eternity future (2 Thess. 1:10; Rev. 5:9; 21:23). The Lord Jesus is magnified in our lives as we humbly follow (Ps. 23:3; Matt. 5:16; 1 Cor. 10:31; 1 Pet. 1:7; 4:10–11) and boldly proclaim him (1 Pet. 2:9).

Week 7: A Parting Plea

1 Thessalonians 5:12–28

The Place of the Passage

Having discussed our hope in 1 Thessalonians 4:13–5:11, Paul now gives a flurry of parting instructions—17 consecutive commands—before concluding the letter with final comments and a benediction.

The Big Picture

The final verses of this letter feature an array of brief yet profound exhortations for the family of God in Thessalonica.

Read through the complete passage for this study, 1 Thessalonians 5:12–28. Then review the questions below concerning this concluding section of 1 Thessalonians and write your notes on them. (For further background, see the *ESV Study Bible*, page 2311; available online at www.esv.org.)

How many times in this closing section of the letter does Paul address his readers as "brothers"? Based on other New Testament references to the church as God's family (e.g., Matt. 12:48–50; Eph. 2:19; 1 Tim. 3:15), what can you discern about God's design for the church?

In 1 Thessalonians 5:12–13, what are Paul's two instructions for how church members are to relate to their pastors or elders? How does your culture's view of authority differ from the Bible's view of authority?

In verse 12, Paul observes that the Thessalonians' pastors are both "among" and "over" them. Why is this significant, and how do these two aspects of spiritual leadership counterbalance each other? What happens in a church when the "among you" emphasis begins to drown out the "over you" emphasis? What about the reverse?

In verse 13, Paul tells the Thessalonians to respect and esteem their pastors "very highly *in love*." This is a vital qualifier, for it is possible to respect or esteem others without loving them (e.g., a gifted politician). It is also possible to love someone without respecting or esteeming them (e.g., a difficult family member). What is one way you can begin to respect and esteem your church leaders with more intentionality and love?

To whom are the commands in 1 Thessalonians 5:14 addressed? Likewise, according to Ephesians 4:12–13, who is humanly responsible for doing the "work of ministry" in the church? Does this surprise you?

It is possible that the commands in 1 Thessalonians 5:14 correspond to previous discussions in the letter: "admonish the idle" to 4:11–12; "encourage the fainthearted" to 4:13–18; and "help the weak" to 4:1–8. What can we learn about the breadth of ministry—and the wisdom it requires—from these commands?

Of all the commands in this section, which challenges you most? Why? How might you more deliberately cultivate a heart posture of obedience in this area?

Twice now Paul has directly answered the popular question, "What is God's will for my life?" What was his first response (see 4:3)? What is his second (5:18)? Thinking of your own circumstances, what might it look like for you to carry out God's will based on these two verses?

Where does the Trinity appear in 5:12–28, and why is this significant?

Although gospel-believing Christians disagree on the nature of the "prophecies" in verses 19–22, what is clear is that we are to "test everything" we hear, especially words claiming divine origin. According to John Stott, we ought to subject such claims to five tests: (1) the truth of Scripture (Acts 17:11); (2) the nature of Christ (1 John 4:1–3; see also 1 Cor. 12:3; 2 John 9–10); (3) the gospel of grace (Gal. 1:6–9); (4) the character of the speaker (Matt. 7:15–20); and (5) the edification of the body (1 Corinthians 14). Which of these tests are you most inclined to value? Which are you inclined to overlook?

In Paul's benediction (1 Thess. 5:23–24), he prays for the church's sanctification as if it were a gift. Back in 4:1–7, however, he discussed sanctification as if it were a calling. Which is it? Is our increasing conformity to Christ *our* responsibility (4:1–7) or *God's* (5:23–24)?

Read through the following three sections on *Gospel Glimpses, Whole-Bible Connections*, and *Theological Soundings*. Then take time to consider the *Personal Implications* these sections may have for you.

Gospel Glimpses

BROTHERS. This word appears five times in this final section of 1 Thessalonians, spotlighting the unique relationship enjoyed by Christians in general and fellow local church members[1] in particular. Language denoting our sibling status in the family of God is not sentimental spiritual talk; it is at the white-hot center of the gospel. We have not always enjoyed this standing, after all. Our Maker once stood against us because of our sin. But through reliance on Jesus, our Judge has become our Father. Believers now have the same Father precisely because we have the same Savior—we are sons of God through union with the Son of God. As J. I. Packer writes in his classic book *Knowing God*, "'Father' is the Christian name for God. Our understanding of Christianity cannot be better than our grasp of adoption. To be right with God the Judge is a great thing, but to be loved and cared for by God the Father is greater" (201). The difference between justification and adoption, then, is the difference between a courtroom and living room. If justification is God's declaring us righteous, adoption is God's declaring us *his*.

GRACE. Final words are significant, and the end of 1 Thessalonians is no exception: "The grace of our Lord Jesus Christ be with you" (5:28). Do you recall how the letter began? "Grace to you and peace" (1:1). This framing is not accidental. Paul is ending where he started, and implying that everything in between—all 87 verses—are to be interpreted and applied in light of the bookends. What is the nature of the grace Paul prays would be *with* the Thessalonians amid their trials (5:28)? It is "the grace of our Lord Jesus Christ"—God's unevoked, unmerited favor purchased with the currency of his Son's blood. This grace is free for us, but it was infinitely costly for Christ.

Whole-Bible Connections

REPAY EVIL WITH GOOD. Old Testament law had enshrined a principle of retributive justice known as *lex talionis*; the punishment inflicted should correspond in degree and kind to the offense of the wrongdoer: "If there is harm, then you shall pay life for life, eye for eye, tooth for tooth, hand for hand, foot for foot, burn for burn, wound for wound, stripe for stripe" (Ex. 21:23–25; see also Lev. 24:17–22; Deut. 19:21). This was to limit revenge and vendettas. Yet, in the Sermon on the Mount Jesus declared, "You have heard that it was said, 'An eye for an eye and a tooth for a tooth.' But I say to you, Do not resist the one who is evil. But if anyone slaps you on the right cheek, turn to him the other also" (Matt. 5:38–39; see also 5:40–42). Jesus was not abolishing the law but rather going to its heart—love—in order to establish a radical new command (Rom. 13:8–10; Gal. 5:14; James 2:8). Citizens of his kingdom, he insisted, are to love their enemies and pray for their persecutors (Matt. 5:44)—unlike citizens of the world, who love only their friends (Matt. 5:46–47). Paul's commands in 1 Thessalonians 5:15 to repay none with evil and to pursue all with good, then, are applications of our Lord's own words. Indeed, the New Testament is filled with Jesus-echoing demands to do what is impossible without him—blessing persecutors, resisting revenge, and overcoming evil with good (e.g., Rom. 12:14–21).

Theological Soundings

FRUIT OF THE SPIRIT. Written around AD 51, 1 Thessalonians is probably Paul's second-earliest New Testament letter. His earliest is Galatians, written a few years prior (c. AD 48). In that letter Paul lists the fruit of the Spirit, against which "there is no law" (Gal. 5:22–23). Interestingly, in the final section of 1 Thessalonians he again highlights more than half of them: love (5:13), joy (5:16), peace (5:13, 23), patience (5:14), goodness (5:15), and, on the part of God, faithfulness (5:24). This makes sense, given the letter's emphasis on holiness and sanctification (see especially 4:1–7), right up to the final prayer (5:23–24).

WISDOM. Although this word does not appear in this passage, our need for wisdom is evident: "We urge you, brothers, admonish the idle, encourage the fainthearted, help the weak, be patient with them all" (5:14). Paul is a physician of souls, prescribing different medicines for different maladies, and he expects ordinary church members to do the same. Discerning which kind of person you are ministering to (and thus which "medicine" is needed) requires profound wisdom—the skill of applying the principles of Scripture to the complexities of life. Daily living hinges heavily on such situational wisdom—figuring out what to do in the countless circumstances where simple moral rules do not immediately or obviously apply. Thankfully, God has given us an entire literary genre in Scripture (wisdom literature[2]) devoted to making us wiser. And in the New Testament we encounter the embodiment of divine wisdom himself, Jesus Christ (Matt. 12:42; 1 Cor. 1:24, 30; Col. 2:2–3), who rescues arrogant fools and makes them wise (1 Cor. 1:18–31). Biblical wisdom is evidenced in action (Matt. 11:19), is vital for witness (Col. 4:5), and is received through prayer (James 1:5). Its character is "pure, then peaceable, gentle, open to reason, full of mercy and good fruits, impartial and sincere" (James 3:17). In other words, wisdom looks like Jesus.

Personal Implications

Take time to reflect on the implications of 1 Thessalonians 5:12–28 for your own life today. Consider what you have learned that might lead you to praise God, repent of sin, and trust in his gracious promises. Make notes below on the personal applications for your walk with the Lord based on the (1) *Gospel Glimpses*, (2) *Whole-Bible Connections*, (3) *Theological Soundings*, and (4) this passage as a whole.

1. Gospel Glimpses

2. Whole-Bible Connections

3. Theological Soundings

4. 1 Thessalonians 5:12–28

As You Finish This Unit . . .

Take a moment now to ask for the Lord's blessing and help as you conclude this study of 1 Thessalonians. And take a moment also to look back through this unit of study and reflect on some key lessons the Lord may be teaching you.

Definitions

[1] **Church member** – A Christian who obeys God by formally committing to a local congregation. God designed our discipleship to be anchored in a church, with our lives submitted to the oversight of elders and to the care and accountability of fellow members.

[2] **Wisdom literature** – A genre of biblical books including Job, Psalms, Proverbs, Ecclesiastes, and Song of Solomon.

Week 8: Overview of 2 Thessalonians

Still in Corinth on his second missionary journey[1] (Acts 18:1–18), the apostle Paul sits down to write a follow-up letter to the Thessalonian church some 360 miles (by land) to the north. We know this is not his first correspondence with the congregation he helped to plant (see Acts 17:1–11), for he references a previous letter (almost certainly 1 Thessalonians) in 2:15. In that epistle—the earliest in the New Testament after Galatians and James—he had covered a number of pressing topics in light of Timothy's report (1 Thess. 3:6). Although roughly half the length of 1 Thessalonians—three chapters compared to five and 47 verses compared to 89—2 Thessalonians is packed with theological insight and practical significance.

The apparent occasion for 2 Thessalonians is an update Paul has received concerning the church (2 Thess. 3:11). Three issues in particular demand further instruction and application: (1) the ongoing experience of persecution (see 1 Thess. 1:6; 2:14; 3:1–5); (2) an unsettling rumor concerning the day of the Lord (see 1 Thess. 5:1–11); and (3) the ongoing presence of idlers among the church (see 1 Thess. 4:11–12; 5:14). Second Thessalonians broadly addresses these themes in chapters 1, 2, and 3, respectively.

It is fascinating to note that the title "Lord Jesus" appears 12 times in this three-chapter letter—more than in any other New Testament epistle. (The title appears 11 times in 1 Thessalonians.) Paul remains intent on spotlighting Jesus' lordship over human history as well as over our individual lives. (For further background, see the *ESV Study Bible*, pages 2313–2315; available online at www.esv.org.)

▶ Placing 2 Thessalonians in the Larger Story

Only two decades have passed since Jesus of Nazareth—Messiah of Israel, Savior of the world, eternal Son of God—completed his earthly mission by means of his atoning[2] death, victorious resurrection, and royal ascension. In the meantime, a man named Paul has been dramatically converted on the road to Damascus (Acts 9:1–19) and commissioned as an apostle to proclaim Christ and plant churches. In Acts 17:1–11 we read of his ministry in—and banishment from—the city of Thessalonica. It is this congregation in Macedonia (northern Greece) that he now addresses for the second time from Corinth (southern Greece), having received a new report about them (2 Thess. 3:11).

▶ Key Passage

"We ought always to give thanks to God for you, brothers beloved by the Lord, because God chose you as the firstfruits to be saved, through sanctification by the Spirit and belief in the truth. To this he called you through our gospel, so that you may obtain the glory of our Lord Jesus Christ." (2 Thess. 2:13–14)

▶ Date and Historical Background

In Acts 17:1–11, Luke recounts Paul's visit to Thessalonica and ministry among its synagogues. Nearing the end of his second missionary journey, Paul is in Corinth for 18 months (Acts 18:1–18) when he writes to the Thessalonian church. (See Week 1 for more details to the backstory.)

Thessalonica was the capital of the Roman province of Macedonia, in northern Greece. Boasting a population of more than 100,000, the city was a powerful commercial center situated on the Aegean seacoast along the Via Egnatia (a major Roman east-west highway). Given its geographical and cultural position, Thessalonica was a hotbed of lucrative trade and religious pluralism. While primarily devoted to the pantheon of Greco-Roman gods, the city also included a substantial contingent of Diaspora[3] Jews—as evidenced by Paul's focus on the local synagogue (Acts 17:1–4, 10).

Outline

IV. Opening (1:1–2)

V. Thanksgiving and Comfort for the Persecuted Thessalonians (1:3–12)

   A. Thanksgiving proper (1:3–4)
   B. Justice guaranteed when Jesus returns (1:5–10)
   C. Prayer report (1:11–12)

VI. Refuting the False Claim about the Day of the Lord (2:1–17)

   A. The false claim (2:1–2)
   B. The false claim refuted (2:3–12)
   C. Reassurance (2:13–14)
   D. Exhortation (2:15)
   E. Prayer (2:16–17)

VII. Transition (3:1–5)

   A. Request for prayer (3:1–2)
   B. Reassurance (3:3–4)
   C. Prayer (3:5)

VIII. The Problem of the Idlers (3:6–15)

   A. The command to the community (3:6)
   B. The tradition (3:7–10)
   C. The problem (3:11)
   D. The command to the idlers (3:12)
   E. Instructions to the community (3:13–15)

IX. Conclusion (3:16–18)

As You Get Started

As we begin this study, do you have a sense of any specific emphases of 2 Thessalonians? Without using your Bible, do any passages from 2 Thessalonians come to mind? Has this letter already been meaningful to your walk with the Lord in any specific ways?

Do a quick read-through of 2 Thessalonians. What themes or topics stand out? What about particular words or phrases? Write them down. What would you say is Paul's primary aim in this letter?

How would you describe the contributions of 2 Thessalonians to Christian theology? What do you think the letter teaches us about Jesus, sin, salvation, the end times, or any other doctrine?

What aspects of 2 Thessalonians have confused you? Are there any specific questions you hope to resolve through studying this letter?

As You Finish This Unit . . .

Take a few minutes to ask God to bless you with increased understanding and a transformed heart and life as you begin this study of 2 Thessalonians.

Definitions

[1] **Missionary journey** – The book of Acts recounts at least three strategic journeys in Paul's ministry: (1) his first journey, Acts 13:4–14:26 (c. AD 46–47); (2) his second journey, 15:35–18:22 (c. 48/49–51); (3) his third journey, 18:22–21:17 (c. 52–57). Paul wrote 1–2 Thessalonians from Corinth during his second journey.

[2] **Atonement** – The sacrifice of Jesus on the cross as a substitute for sinners. In joyful obedience to the will of his Father (Heb. 12:2), Jesus was punished in the place of his people, all who repent of sin and rely on him.

[3] **Diaspora** – Also known as the Dispersion, the term refers to the historical scattering of Jews from Jerusalem into the rest of the Mediterranean world. Although applicable to Jewish persons in general (John 7:35), the NT chiefly applies such language to the scattering of Jewish Christians in particular. Luke highlights the Diaspora's origins in persecution (Acts 8:1–4; 11:19), and both James and Peter address letters to believers "in the Dispersion" (James 1:1; 1 Pet. 1:1).

WEEK 9: THE AFFLICTERS AND THE AFFLICTED

2 Thessalonians 1:1–12

The Place of the Passage

Paul opens his second letter to the Thessalonians (the first letter is referenced in 2 Thess. 2:15) in typical fashion, with an introductory greeting (vv. 1–2) and a statement of gratitude for God's grace in the church's life (vv. 3–4) before launching into the body of the letter (vv. 5–12). His pastoral heart is on display as he seeks to comfort his readers with a vision of their future. King Jesus will surely return to judge their enemies and grant them endless relief and joy.

The Big Picture

In 2 Thessalonians 1:1–12, Paul greets the church, commends them for embodying God's grace, and reminds them of Christ's promised return to punish their persecutors and grant them unending rest.

> ### Reflection and Discussion

Read through the complete text for this study, 2 Thessalonians 1:1–12. Then review the questions below concerning this opening passage of 2 Thessalonians and record your responses. (For further background, see the *ESV Study Bible*, pages 2316–2317; available online at www.esv.org.)

1. Greeting and Gratitude (1:1–4)

In verse 3, Paul insists that it is "right" to verbalize gratitude to God for the Thessalonians. Why do you think he uses this word? What does this imply about ingratitude?

How do the virtues and characteristics Paul identifies in verses 3–4 correspond to the ones he highlighted in 1 Thessalonians 1:3 and 5:8?

How does Paul's statement in verse 3 correspond to his prayer for the church in 1 Thessalonians 3:12?

What does it mean to "boast" (v. 4)? What is the difference between this kind of boasting and sinful boasting?

2. A Day of Justice and Mercy (1:5–12)

How does Paul describe God's judgment in verse 5? Is this how you think of it? How does viewing God's judgment this way matter on a practical level?

In the middle of verse 7, Paul turns on a dime from speaking of "God" (vv. 5–7a) to speaking of "the Lord Jesus" (vv. 7b–10). Compare the identity of the one "repaying with affliction" (v. 6) to the identity of the one "inflicting vengeance" (v. 8). What does a careful look at this passage indicate about the nature of the relationship between God and Jesus?

Reread Paul's description of Christ's return in 1 Thessalonians 4:13–18. How does that passage compare to 2 Thessalonians 1:5–12? Is Paul referring to the same event or different ones?

What do we learn about the nature of hell from verse 9?

According to verse 10, for whom is Jesus returning, and by what criteria are they identified? Given this description, is he coming back for *you*?

What happens to our every "resolve for good" and "work of faith" (v. 11) if we remove God from the equation? How should the language of Paul's prayerful challenge in verses 11–12 shape our perspective on the relationship between God's work and ours? What effect should this have on our hearts?

How do verses 2 and 12 frame chapter 1? Why is this significant?

Read through the following three sections on *Gospel Glimpses, Whole-Bible Connections*, and *Theological Soundings*. Then take time to consider the *Personal Implications* these sections may have for you.

Gospel Glimpses

OBEY THE GOSPEL. Paul speaks of those who "do not obey the gospel of our Lord Jesus" (2 Thess. 1:8). This is intriguing, since "obey" is not the typical imperative associated with our gospel response (but see Rom. 10:16 and 1 Pet. 4:17). Obeying the gospel means embracing it, submitting to it, and responding gladly to its inherent demand to repent and believe in King Jesus. Sometimes this demand is explicit (e.g., Acts 20:21); other times it is implied. The notion of obeying the gospel also has implications for how we conduct evangelism.[1] In 1 Thessalonians 2, it is interesting that Paul's shorthand for "we [declared] to you the gospel" (v. 2) is simply "our appeal" (v. 3). This is because evangelism is inherently persuasive (see 2 Cor. 5:11, 20). If you have not yet implored someone to repent and believe, then your evangelism—your "gospeling"—is not yet complete.

Whole-Bible Connections

DIVINE RETRIBUTION. While taking vengeance is not appropriate for Christ's people (see "Whole-Bible Connections" for 1 Thessalonians 5:12–28), the Old Testament concept of proportional repayment or retributive justice is entirely right for a God of righteousness who never overreacts and whose punishment always fits the crime. God's people can take comfort in knowing that he sides with them, identifies with them, will fight for them, and will win. Ever since God's covenant promise to Abraham that "him who dishonors you I will curse" (Gen. 12:3), the Scriptures pulse with the conviction that God takes his people's persecution personally and will repay their afflicters with justice (see, e.g., Ex. 23:22; Deut. 30:7; Ps. 137:8; Jer. 25:14; 30:20; 46:10; 50:15, 28–29; 51:6, 11, 24, 36, 56; Ezek. 35:15; Joel 3:4, 7; Obad. 15; Hab. 2:8). In 2 Thessalonians 1, Paul assures the beleaguered church that God will "repay with affliction" their afflicters (v. 6) by means of his vengeance-inflicting Son (vv. 7–8). It is significant that Paul, without embarrassment or explanation, applies Old Testament language for Yahweh directly to Jesus. The man from Nazareth will mediate heaven's justice on behalf of those for whom he died.

Theological Soundings

KINGDOM OF GOD. Referenced in 1:5, God's "kingdom" is the realm of his redemptive reign. It refers not only to his geographical ownership but also to his comprehensive rule. His king*dom*, then, is a function of his king*ship*. And God's kingdom is inescapably tied to salvation. Regrettably, many who define the kingdom without reference to God's saving activity in Christ propose a definition any theist[2]—such as a Jew or a Muslim—could support, but God's kingdom is inseparably tied to God's King (Matt. 4:17; Mark 1:15; Luke 17:21; John 18:36). Although Old Testament precedent for the kingdom certainly exists (e.g., Dan. 2:44; 7:14, 18, 23, 27; Isa. 9:2ff.; 11:1ff.; 24:23; Zeph. 3:15; Zech. 14:9ff.; Obad. 21; Amos 9:11ff.), it is the arrival of Jesus that is presented as the arrival of the kingdom. This is why we say that God's kingdom is both a present (e.g., Matt. 3:2; 4:17; 10:7; 11:11–12; 12:28; 13:41) and a future (e.g., Matt. 6:10; 8:11; 13:43; 16:28; 18:1–4; 19:24–25; 25:31, 34; 26:29) reality. Jesus inaugurated it when he came, and he will consummate it when he returns. Although God's kingdom extends over every square inch of his universe, it is uniquely present where his Son is uniquely present—that is, in the church. God has given the local church the "keys of the kingdom" to declare on heaven's behalf the identity of those who belong to Jesus (see Matt 16:16–19; 18:17–20; 28:18–20). Every local church is a colony of the kingdom—an embassy of heaven on earth. Ultimately, the clearest picture of "kingdom life" is seen in the final chapters of Revelation, where the fullness of God's kingdom unilaterally and climactically descends as a new heaven and a new earth (21:1–5).

ETERNAL DESTRUCTION. According to verse 9, the "destruction" of the condemned will not be momentary but "eternal." Hell will be every bit as eternal as heaven will be (e.g., note the parallel between "eternal punishment" and "eternal life" in Matt. 25:46). Indeed, this sentence of God's endless justice (see 1 Thess. 1:10; 5:9; Rom. 2:5) is fair and right. "Shall not the Judge of all the earth do what is just?" (Gen. 18:25; see also 2 Thess. 1:5; 2 Tim. 4:8). However, those who know God (1 Thess. 1:8)—who obey the gospel (v. 8) by trusting the Son (v. 10)—will be saved from this deserved verdict. And saved persons will anticipate and "marvel at" (2 Thess. 1:10; see also 2 Tim. 4:8) their beautiful Redeemer's return.

Personal Implications

Take time to reflect on the implications of 2 Thessalonians 1:1–12 for your own life today. Consider what you have learned that might lead you to praise God, repent of sin, and trust in his gracious promises. Make notes below on the personal applications for your walk with the Lord based on the (1) *Gospel Glimpses*, (2) *Whole-Bible Connections*, (3) *Theological Soundings*, and (4) this passage as a whole.

1. Gospel Glimpses

2. Whole-Bible Connections

3. Theological Soundings

4. 2 Thessalonians 1:1–12

> ### As You Finish This Unit . . .

Take a moment now to ask for the Lord's blessing and help as you continue in this study of 2 Thessalonians. And take a moment also to look back through this unit of study, to reflect on some key things the Lord may be teaching you.

Definitions

[1] **Evangelism** – Declaring the gospel (the evangel) of Jesus the King, in the power of the Spirit, and calling for response—while leaving the results to God.

[2] **Theist** – A person who believes in one or more gods.

WEEK 10: THE MAN OF LAWLESSNESS

2 Thessalonians 2:1–17

▲

The Place of the Passage

Having comforted the church with the promise of King Jesus' return to judge their enemies, Paul continues to focus on the future. First, he must put to rest an unsettling rumor that the day of the Lord has already occurred (2 Thess. 2:1–2). In the process of refuting this false claim (2:3–12), he highlights a coming event ("the rebellion") and a coming person ("the man of lawlessness"), both of which must appear before that final day. Paul concludes the chapter with thanksgiving (2:13–14), exhortation (2:15), and prayer (2:16–17).

The Big Picture

In 2 Thessalonians 2:1–17, Paul refutes a troubling claim that the day of the Lord has already come, and he summons the church to stand firm and cling to truth.

> ## Reflection and Discussion

Read through the complete passage for this study, 2 Thessalonians 2:1–17. Then review the questions below on this section of 2 Thessalonians and record your notes and reflections. (For further background, see the *ESV Study Bible*, pages 2317–2318; available online at www.esv.org.)

1. The Man and the Mystery (2:1–12)

Read Matthew 24 and identify several ways in which Paul's words here echo Jesus' own words there.

Some in Thessalonica had grown concerned that the day of the Lord had already come and that they had missed out. Such a fear may strike us as bizarre, but consider the nature of fear. How is it sometimes irrational? How is it sometimes contagious?

In 2 Thessalonians 2:1–12, Paul responds to the fear that the day of the Lord had come too quickly and that living Christians had missed out. How in his previous letter had he responded to the opposite fear—that the day of the Lord was not coming quickly enough and that deceased Christians had missed out?

Verse 5, though easy to skim past, is profoundly important. In the process of refuting a false rumor, Paul appeals to his own authoritative teaching, which the congregation knew and had either forgotten or dismissed. Given that apostolic teaching is now permanently preserved for us in the New Testament, what might be a contemporary application of verse 5 (see also v. 15)?

Which verse in this passage indicates that it is wrong to conclude that the "man of lawlessness" is Satan himself?

The promise that Jesus will kill the lawless one "with the breath of his mouth" is an allusion to Isaiah 11:4. He will destroy with his voice—that is, in accordance with his word (see Rev. 19:15). How else does the New Testament apply this messianic[1] passage (Isa. 11:1–5) to Jesus? (See, for example, Romans 15:12; Revelation 5:5; and Revelation 22:16.)

Do you think the man of lawlessness is the same figure as "the antichrist" described by John (see 1 John 2:18, 22; 4:3; 2 John 7)? Why or why not?

Second Thessalonians 2:10 speaks of those who "refused to love the truth and so be saved." Salvation, then, is impossible apart from (1) the truth and (2) love for the truth. What is the significance of the word "love" here? Why do you think Paul chose it instead of, say, "know" or "affirm"? Lastly, how does verse 10 shed light on what it means to "believe the truth" (v. 12)?

As we put verses 10 and 12 together, a vital truth begins to emerge: Behind an unconvinced mind lies a hard heart. People ultimately reject the gospel for moral, not intellectual, reasons. How do the following verses confirm this biblical picture: Psalm 119:100–104; Mark 6:52; 8:17; John 3:18–19; Romans 1:18; Ephesians 4:17–18?

In contrast to those who are "perishing" (v. 10) and "condemned" (v. 12), Paul tells the Thessalonians that God "chose" them to be saved (v. 13). Spend a few minutes pondering Deuteronomy 7:7–8 and Ephesians 1:4–5. Contrary to common assumption, how is the doctrine of election—which Paul introduced to the church at the outset of his first letter (1 Thess. 1:4–5)—a love doctrine?

2. Stand Firm and Hold Tight (2:13–17)

Paul's words of thanksgiving in verses 13–14 are not the stuff of shallow religious jargon. Which persons of the Trinity does he mention, and what roles are they fulfilling? Also, where in these verses do you see the moment of justification? The process of sanctification? The promise of glorification?

God offers us comfort that is "eternal" and hope that is "good" (v. 16). What does this imply about the type of comfort and hope that the world offers? How have you experienced this contrast in your own life?

Read through the following three sections on *Gospel Glimpses, Whole-Bible Connections*, and *Theological Soundings*. Then take time to consider the *Personal Implications* these sections may have for you.

Gospel Glimpses

DIVINE ELECTION. "God chose you as the firstfruits to be saved" (2 Thess. 2:13). Every Bible-believing Christian acknowledges the reality of "election" or "predestination," since those are words found in the Bible. Debate centers not on the *existence* of divine election, then, but on its *nature*. Is God's election "conditional" (based on a foreseen human condition, such as faith) or "unconditional" (not based on any foreseen condition, including faith). Scripture's overwhelming witness is that God, out of sheer mercy and love, chooses or elects unconditionally—not based on any prior condition (such as faith or merit). Faith is the consequence of election, not the cause of it. In other words, we were not chosen because we would believe; we believed because we were chosen (note carefully the order in texts like John 10:26 and Acts 13:48). Moreover, we owe our regeneration to *God's* will, not ours (John 1:12–13). Jesus himself testified to the sovereignty[2] of the Father (John 6:44, 65), of the Son (Matt. 11:27; John 5:21; 15:16), and the Spirit (John 3:6) in human salvation. Little wonder, then, that the theme of election shines in many Trinitarian texts (e.g., 2 Thess. 2:13; see also 1 Thess. 1:4–5; Eph. 1:3–14; 1 Pet. 1:1–2). Unlike election, salvation *is* conditional. Yet even the necessary conditions—repentance (Acts 5:31; 11:18; 2 Tim. 2:25–26) and faith (Acts 18:27; Eph. 2:8; Phil. 1:29; 1 Tim. 1:14)—are gifts of God's grace that can never be lost. Because of this, God gets all of the glory for our salvation. And far from hindering our need for prayer or evangelism, election is designed to empower it (see, e.g., Acts 18:9–10; 2 Tim. 2:10; Titus 1:1).

Whole-Bible Connections

ABOMINATION OF DESOLATION. Although not mentioned explicitly, this abomination seems to be the relevant event in 2 Thessalonians 2:1–12. Daniel had prophesied about Antiochus Epiphanes IV, the blasphemous Syrian king who desecrated the temple by sacrificing a pig in the Most Holy Place in 164 BC (see Dan. 9:27; 11:36–37; 12:11). Referencing this event, Jesus explained what to do "when you see the abomination of desolation spoken of by the prophet Daniel, standing in the holy place" (Matt. 24:15). Daniel's prophecy, then, found initial fulfillment in the life of Antiochus Epiphanes IV and further fulfillment in the destruction of the temple (and accompanying acts of sacrilege) in AD 70. In 2 Thessalonians 2:1–12, Paul is likely speaking of a still-future moment in which the man of lawlessness will, in a concrete act of defiance, seek to deify himself in God's temple (perhaps a reference to the new covenant church; see 1 Cor. 3:16–17; Eph. 2:21–22; 1 Pet. 2:5).

TEMPLE OF GOD. The man of lawlessness will exalt himself in "the temple of God" (2 Thess. 2:4). The temple is a major theme that develops throughout the storyline of Scripture. God's temple is his sanctuary—the place on earth where his presence uniquely dwells. God installed Adam as a priest-king to rule and guard his original temple-sanctuary in Eden (Gen. 1:28; 2:15). Adam failed, however, and was exiled from his presence. God later chose and commissioned Israel to be a "kingdom of priests" (Ex. 19:6) who would meet with God first in the tabernacle and later in the Jerusalem temple. Like Adam, however, Israel failed and was exiled from his presence. With their temple in ruins, the banished nation's hopes focused on a future end-time temple (Ezekiel 40–48). When the fullness of time had come, the eternal Word himself came and "tabernacled" among us (John 1:14). Jesus explicitly referred to himself as God's temple (John 2:19–22) and, remarkably, succeeded where both Adam and Israel had failed. Today, all those united to Jesus by faith are God's new temple—the place where his Spirit resides individually (1 Cor. 6:19) and, above all, corporately (1 Cor. 3:16; Eph. 2:21–22; 1 Pet. 2:5). And one day we will be ushered into God's very presence, where he and the Lamb will be the temple (Rev. 21:22). In fact, the dimensions of the new Jerusalem are cubic, signifying that the entire city will be a Most Holy Place (see 1 Kings 6:20; Rev. 21:16)—a new creation filled with the glory of the Lord as the waters cover the sea.

Theological Soundings

FALSE TEACHING. Energized by Satan, the "lawless" one will perform "false signs and wonders" (2 Thess. 2:9), resulting in widespread "deception" (2:10). He will not be boring; he will be captivating, impressive, spectacular. And his forerunners—those embodying "the mystery of lawlessness" (2:7)—will be all these things as well. False teachers, after all, are not only dynamic people; they are often nice. It is little wonder, then, that the Old Testament repeatedly warns against false prophets and false shepherds (e.g., Jer. 23:16–17, 21–22; Ezek. 13:10; 34:1–7). Jesus calls such persons "wolves" (Matt. 7:15–20; 10:16; John 10:12–13), as does Paul (Acts 20:28–31). These imposters are masters of deceit; indeed, the only things more dangerous than wolves who look like wolves are wolves who look like sheep. Hence Paul warns of "false apostles" and "deceitful workmen" disguised as apostles of Christ (2 Cor. 11:13). Jesus promised that Satan's mouthpieces would be numerous and successful: "Many false prophets will arise and lead many astray. . . . [They will] perform great signs and wonders, so as to lead astray, if possible, even the elect" (Matt. 24:11, 24; see also 1 John 4:1). The Devil's attacks are often doctrinal; he attacks the church by targeting her teaching: "The time is coming when people will not endure sound teaching, but having itching ears they will accumulate for themselves teachers to suit their own passions, and will turn away from listening to the truth and wander off into myths" (2 Tim. 4:3–4; see also 1 Tim. 4:1; 2 Pet. 2:1; 1 John 2:18, 22; 4:3; 2 John 7). Besides indwelling sin, there may be no greater threat to God's people than false teaching (see, e.g., 1 Tim. 1:3–7; 6:3–5; 2 Pet. 2:1–22; Jude 3–19).

DIVINE COMFORT. "Now may our Lord Jesus Christ himself, and God our Father, who loved us and gave us eternal comfort . . . comfort your hearts" (2 Thess. 2:16–17). Ever since humanity's revolt in Eden, evil and suffering have been near—painfully, hauntingly, inescapably near. We live and move and have our being in the valley of the shadow of death. Where, then, do we turn for relief, for assurance, for security, for calm? The Bible is clear: God alone is the only reliable source of comfort amid the sadness of this life. Scripture's most famous psalm rings with the assurance that "your rod and your staff, they comfort me" (Ps. 23:4). Such acknowledgments—and promises—of God's comfort pervade the pages of God's Word (e.g., Pss. 71:21; 86:17; 119:76; Isa. 51:3, 12; 52:9; 66:13; Jer. 31:13). As Jesus himself declared, "Blessed are those who mourn, for they shall be comforted" (Matt. 5:4). The Christian is not immune from pain but intimately knows the "God of all comfort" (2 Cor. 1:3), who consoles the downcast (2 Cor. 1:4; 2 Cor. 7:6). It is striking that, out of all the words Jesus could have used to describe the Holy Spirit he would send, he chose *paraklētos*—"Helper" or "Comforter" (John 14:26; see also Acts 9:31). This designation assumes that life in this age will be filled to the brim with grief, but that the Christian will never be abandoned (Matt. 28:20; Heb. 13:15).

> ### Personal Implications

Take time to reflect on the implications of 2 Thessalonians 2:1–17 for your own life today. Consider what you have learned that might lead you to praise God, repent of sin, and trust in his gracious promises. Make notes below on the personal applications

for your walk with the Lord based on the (1) *Gospel Glimpses*, (2) *Whole-Bible Connections*, (3) *Theological Soundings*, and (4) this passage as a whole.

1. Gospel Glimpses

2. Whole-Bible Connections

3. Theological Soundings

4. 2 Thessalonians 2:1–17

As You Finish This Unit . . .

Take a moment now to ask for the Lord's blessing and help as you continue in this study of 2 Thessalonians. And take a moment also to look back through this unit of study and reflect on some key lessons the Lord may be teaching you.

Definitions

[1] **Messianic** – Promises pertaining to Israel's Messiah. "Messiah" or "Christ" means "anointed one" and refers to Israel's long-awaited King who would accomplish salvation and establish justice on her behalf. The NT reveals that Jesus of Nazareth is the Christ, the Son of the living God.

[2] **Sovereignty** – Supreme power and authority. God is the only being in the universe who is in charge of everything (1 Tim. 6:15–16); indeed, his sovereignty is comprehensive (Ps. 115:3) and meticulous (Prov. 16:33). He directs all things to fulfill his purposes (Job 42:2; Rom. 8:28–29; Eph. 1:11).

WEEK 11: THE
IDLE PROBLEM

2 Thessalonians 3:1–18

The Place of the Passage

If persecutors were the primary problem behind chapter 1 and false teachers the problem behind chapter 2, idlers or loafers are the problem in chapter 3. After requesting prayer and giving assurance to the Thessalonians in light of God's faithfulness (2 Thess. 3:1–5), Paul transitions to warn those in the church who are refusing to work (vv. 6–15). He then concludes the letter with a benediction[1] and personal farewell (vv. 16–18).

The Big Picture

In 2 Thessalonians 3:1–18, Paul takes up one final issue present in the church: the sin of idleness (vv. 6–15). His discussion is prefaced by words of assurance (vv. 1–5) and concluded with words of blessing (vv. 16–18).

Read through 2 Thessalonians 3:1–18, the passage for this week's study. Then review the following questions, recording your responses and taking notes on this final section of this letter. (For further background, see the *ESV Study Bible*, pages 2319–2320; available online at www.esv.org.)

1. Prayer and Promise (3:1–5)

For what two things does Paul request prayer in verses 1–2? In what sense has verse 1 already "happened among [them]" (see, e.g., 1 Thess. 1:4–5; 2:13). And who, in this context, are the "wicked and evil men" mentioned in verse 2?

In verse 1, Paul likens the word of God to a victorious runner. Perhaps Psalm 147:15 is echoing in his head: "He sends out his command to the earth; his word runs swiftly." Luke uses similar personification[2] at several points throughout Acts (e.g., Acts 6:7; 12:24; 19:20). What does such language suggest about the nature of God's word?

2. A Word to Loafers (3:6–15)

How many times does the word "command" appear in this chapter? Why do you think Paul keeps using such a strong word?

What kind of "tradition" had the Thessalonians "received" (v. 6)? See also 1 Thessalonians 1:6; 2:13; 4:1; 2 Thessalonians 2:5, 15.

Verse 8 is not Paul's first reference to his example of tireless labor. Where in his first letter did he draw attention to his work-related conduct?

In verses 8–9, is Paul saying that it is wrong to receive payment for gospel ministry? (See also 1 Cor. 9:3–14; 2 Cor. 11:7–9; Gal. 6:6; 1 Tim. 5:17–18.) What was the nature of his "right" (3:9), and what was his motivation for relinquishing it (see 1 Thess. 2:9)?

Paul lifts up his team as "an example to imitate" (v. 9). Earlier he had commended the Thessalonians for becoming "imitators of us and of the Lord" (1 Thess. 1:6). Can you think of anywhere else in the New Testament where Christians are called to imitate God? What about imitating other Christians?

At the end of his first letter, Paul had instructed the church to "admonish the idle" (1 Thess. 5:14). Here in 2 Thessalonians 3:6–15 he zooms in on this issue, since it obviously remained a problem (see v. 11). How does Scripture's wisdom literature help us understand the nature and dangers of idleness (e.g., Prov. 6:6–11; 10:4–5; 19:15; 21:25–26; 24:30–34; 26:13–16; 31:27; Eccles. 10:18)? What do we learn about idleness from the teaching of Jesus (Matt. 25:14–30)?

In which area of life are you most tempted toward idleness? Take a moment to identify any disordered desires and false beliefs that may give rise to this tendency in your life. How does the gospel counteract the idolatry that leads to idleness?

It seems likely that 2 Thessalonians 3:14–15 refers to a final stage in the process of church discipline, just short of excommunication (since the offender in view is still considered a "brother"). What warrants exclusion from church membership, according to Jesus and Paul (Matt. 18:15–20; 1 Cor. 5:1–13)? What is the ultimate goal of formal church discipline (2 Cor. 2:6–8)?

----

3. Peace and Grace (3:16–18)

Why do you think Paul concludes this letter with an emphasis on the Lord's peace and presence (v. 16)?

Read through the following three sections on *Gospel Glimpses*, *Whole-Bible Connections*, and *Theological Soundings*. Then take time to consider the *Personal Implications* these sections may have for you.

Gospel Glimpses

FAITH. Paul has the audacity to link the presence of evil with the absence of faith (2 Thess. 3:2). Lack of faith is not innocuous; it is deadly serious. It prevents a virtuous life (Rom. 14:23; Heb. 11:6) and, most importantly, prevents eternal life. "When the Son of Man comes, will he find faith on earth?" (Luke 18:8). Scripture is clear that faith—active reliance and trust—in Jesus is necessary for salvation. Faith is a divine gift (Acts 18:27; Eph. 2:8; Phil. 1:29; 1 Tim. 1:14) that connects a sinner to the source of divine righteousness, Jesus himself. The blessings that are his by right become ours by grace. Through trusting in him we stand righteous before God the Judge and can enjoy an intimate relationship with God the Father.

Whole-Bible Connections

WORK. The Bible is clear that work is a good gift from a good God. Crafted in the image of a working God (Gen. 2:2–3), humans are designed for labor: "God blessed [Adam and Eve]. And God said to them, 'Be fruitful and multiply and fill the earth and subdue it, and have dominion over the fish of the sea and over the birds of the heavens and over every living thing that moves on the earth.' . . . The Lord God took the man and put him in the garden of Eden to work it and keep it" (Gen. 1:28; 2:15). After the rebellion in Eden, God cursed human work by making it difficult (Gen. 3:17–19; see also Eccles. 2:18–24). The difference between Genesis 2 and Genesis 3, then, is the difference between work and toil. Although our labors are often marked by frustration and fruitlessness, God's people are exhorted to work with faithfulness, diligence, and excellence, for his glory (see, e.g., Eccles. 9:10; Col. 3:23–24; 1 Cor. 10:31; 15:10). In addition to imaging and pleasing our King, work is a vitally significant means of loving our neighbor and advancing the common good. Indeed, because Jesus is alive, our labor for him is never in vain (1 Cor. 15:58; Gal. 6:9); on the contrary, it anticipates the renewal of all things under his eternal rule.

Theological Soundings

PEACE. "Now may the Lord of peace himself give you peace at all times in every way" (2 Thess. 3:16). Rooted in the Hebrew concept of *shalom*, the biblical vision of peace is not simply the absence of conflict but the presence of wholeness and flourishing. The Thessalonians would have seen the empire slogan—*pax romana* ("the peace of Rome")—plastered everywhere in their capital city. The message was plain: "If you want peace, submit to Rome." Yet God's people know that true peace has never been found in a culture or government; it has been discovered, however, by millions in the Lord Jesus. As Paul declares elsewhere, "[Christ] himself is our peace" (Eph. 2:14; see also Mic. 5:5). And as Christ promises in the Sermon on the Mount, "Blessed are the peacemakers, for they shall be called sons of God" (Matt. 5:9). The good news of Christianity is that the Son of God himself came to earth and became the ultimate peacemaker—vertically (Rom. 5:1–2) and horizontally (Rom. 12:18). As ambassadors of this Prince of Peace (Isa. 9:6)—the one who secured peace through his shed blood (Col. 1:20)—we are to be the people who "seek peace and pursue it" (Ps. 34:14; see also 1 Pet. 3:8–12).

CHURCH DISCIPLINE. In 2 Thessalonians 3:13–14 Paul seems to be referring to a late stage in the process of church discipline, just short of excommunication. What is church discipline? In short, Jesus gives churches the authority and obligation to remove from membership and the Lord's table[3] those who will not repent of sin. If membership is a church's formal *affirmation* of one's profession of faith ("We believe your profession to be credible"), discipline—culminating in excommunication—is the formal *removal* of that affirmation ("We no longer believe your profession to be credible"). Since Jesus' bride, the church, is to be marked by repentance, unrepentance disqualifies one from becoming or remaining a church member. Described in passages such as Matthew 18:15–20 and 1 Corinthians 5:1–13, church discipline is spiritually vital because unrepentance is spiritually lethal. It belittles the holiness of God, trivializes the seriousness of sin, undermines the preciousness of the gospel, and confuses all—church and world alike—about what it means to follow Jesus. The ultimate goal of discipline is not retribution but restoration, a beautiful picture of which is seen in 2 Corinthians 2:6–8 (perhaps in reference to the offender from 1 Corinthians 5).

Personal Implications

Take time to reflect on the implications of 2 Thessalonians 3:1–18 for your own life today. Consider what you have learned that might lead you to praise God, repent of sin, and trust in his gracious promises. Make notes below on the personal implications for your walk with the Lord based on the (1) *Gospel Glimpses*, (2) *Whole-Bible Connections*, (3) *Theological Soundings*, and (4) this passage as a whole.

1. Gospel Glimpses

2. Whole-Bible Connections

3. Theological Soundings

4. 2 Thessalonians 3:1–18

> ## As You Finish This Unit . . .

Take a moment now to ask for the Lord's blessing and help as you near the end of this study of 2 Thessalonians. Take a moment also to look back through this unit of study and to reflect on some key lessons the Lord may be teaching you.

Definitions

[1] **Benediction** – A prayer for God's blessing at the end of a letter or a worship gathering. Many NT letters include a benediction.

[2] **Personification** – A figure of speech in which something nonhuman is described in human terms. The Bible personifies nature (Ps. 98:8), wisdom (Prov. 1:20), sin (Gen. 4:7), blood (Heb. 12:24), death (Rom. 6:9), and money (Matt. 6:24), among many other things.

[3] **Lord's table** – A reference to the Lord's Supper, one of two ordinances or sacraments (along with baptism) entrusted to the local church. Jesus instituted this commemorative new covenant meal at the Last Supper (Luke 22:14–23), and Paul discusses its meaning and practice in 1 Corinthians 11:17–34. If baptism is the local church's front door, the Lord's Supper is the family dinner table. If baptism binds one to many, the Lord's Supper makes many one.

WEEK 12: SUMMARY AND CONCLUSION

▲

We conclude our study of 1–2 Thessalonians by summarizing the big picture of God's message through these letters as a whole. Then we will consider several questions in order to reflect on various Gospel Glimpses, Whole-Bible Connections, and Theological Soundings from this entire study.

▶ The Big Picture of 1–2 Thessalonians

Two thousand years have passed since Paul penned these letters. The Roman Empire, and the ancient city of Thessalonica, have been reduced to rubble. You can buy a ticket to tour the ruins. The Greco-Roman gods—once the object of so much worship, devotion, sacrifice, and hope—have been relegated to museums and the occasional Disney film. Meanwhile, Christianity has spread from Jerusalem to Judea and Samaria and the ends of the earth (Acts 1:8).

So much has changed in the world since the Thessalonians assembled to hear these letters from their beloved apostle. Yet, in many ways, little has changed. Are we really so different? We too need encouragement (1 Thess. 1:2–10). We too need integrity (1 Thess. 2:1–16). We too need love (1 Thess. 2:17–3:13). We too need challenge (1 Thess. 4:1–12). We too need hope (1 Thess. 4:13–5:11). We too need virtue (1 Thess. 5:12–28). We too need assurance (2 Thess. 1:1–12). We too need correction (2 Thess. 2:1–12). We too need prayer (2 Thess. 2:13–3:5). We too need prodding (2 Thess. 3:6–15). We too need peace (2 Thess. 3:16). And from beginning to end, we too need grace (1 Thess. 1:1; 5:28; 2 Thess. 1:2; 3:18).

First and Second Thessalonians are among the earliest documents we possess from the inception of the New Testament church. (Only James and Galatians were written earlier.) Yet despite a two-millennia gap, these letters ring with relevance for today. The Thessalonians faced intense opposition for their faith (2 Thess. 1:1–12); many believers worldwide have long experienced the same, and those of us in the West are increasingly catching up. The Thessalonians had grown slack in pursuing holiness (1 Thess. 4:1–7); many of us have too. The Thessalonians were unsettled because they had misunderstood their future hope (1 Thess. 4:13–5:11; 2 Thess. 2:1–17); many of us live with similar misunderstanding. Because we are so seldom heavenly minded, we are of little earthly good.

The world should not see its reflection when it peers into the church. Instead, it should see a kind of life available nowhere else. It should see the grace of Jesus, lavished on humble sinners, embodied in self-giving love. Our unbelieving friends and neighbors are clamoring after things that will never satisfy them. They know neither why they are here nor where they are going. What awaits them beyond the grave is terrifying, not beautiful. First and Second Thessalonians resound with the news that salvation—deliverance from God's wrath through the blood of his Son—is available, for free, to all who will turn to, trust in, and treasure the Lord Jesus. These letters resound with the news that the Holy Spirit has taken up residence in the hearts of Christians, empowering us to walk in a manner worthy of God. And these letters resound with the news that this world is not the way it always will be. One day, King Jesus will split the skies and return for his people, establishing justice and restoring all things.

Together, these two letters form an eight-chapter refutation to the idea that eschatology is impractical. It is not. To study eschatology is to be empowered and encouraged (1 Thess. 4:18; 5:11). Eschatology is also relevant to ethics: Christian virtue does not arise out of nowhere, but is driven by past mercy and is sustained by future hope. If you need "strength for today and bright hope for tomorrow," 1–2 Thessalonians are a gift from God to you.

Gospel Glimpses

We have seen the good news of grace woven throughout 1–2 Thessalonians. Elected in eternity past (1 Thess. 1:4; 2 Thess. 2:13) and secured for eternity future (1 Thess. 1:10; 5:9–10), we owe everything to the one who loved us and gave himself for us. The thrilling news of God's achievement in the life, death, resurrection, and promised return of Jesus is the heartbeat of Christian living—and the heartbeat of these letters.

How has 1–2 Thessalonians brought new clarity to your understanding of God's grace?

Were there any particular passages or themes in 1–2 Thessalonians that brought the gospel home to you in a fresh way?

Whole-Bible Connections

These letters have been rich in whole-Bible themes, even though Paul does not explicitly quote from the Old Testament as much as in some other letters (e.g., Romans or Galatians). With the Old Testament furnishing the backdrop, 1–2 Thessalonians yields fresh clarity on a number of themes that have been developing across the storyline of Scripture.

How has this study of 1–2 Thessalonians helped to fill out your understanding of the biblical storyline of redemption?

Are there any themes emphasized in 1–2 Thessalonians that have caused you to better grasp the Bible's unity?

Have any passages or themes expanded your understanding of the wondrous redemption Jesus provides, which he began at his first coming and will consummate at his return?

What connections between 1–2 Thessalonians and the Old Testament were new to you?

Theological Soundings

Our understanding of Christian theology is greatly enriched through 1–2 Thessalonians. Many doctrines and themes are developed, clarified, and reinforced in these divinely inspired letters. Reflect on the doctrinal themes we have encountered.

Has your theology been refined in any specific ways through this study of 1–2 Thessalonians? How so?

How has your understanding of the nature and character of God been developed or deepened throughout this study?

What unique contributions does 1–2 Thessalonians make toward your understanding of who Jesus is and what he has accomplished through his life, death, and resurrection?

What specifically does 1–2 Thessalonians teach us about the human condition and our need for redemption?

Personal Implications

God gave us 1–2 Thessalonians not simply to gratify our curiosity but to transform our lives. If our study of these letters does not deepen our affection for God and our trust in him, we have been wasting our time. As you reflect on 1–2 Thessalonians as a whole, what implications do you see for your relationship with him?

What personal implications for your life emerge from your reflections on the questions already asked in this week's study concerning Gospel Glimpses, Whole-Bible Connections, and Theological Soundings?

What have you learned as you have studied 1–2 Thessalonians that might lead you to praise God, turn away from sin, and trust more firmly in his promises?

As You Finish Studying 1–2 Thessalonians . . .

We rejoice with you as you finish studying the books of 1–2 Thessalonians! May this study become part of your Christian walk of faith, day by day and week by week throughout all your life. Now we would greatly encourage you to study the Word of God in an ongoing way. To help you as you continue your study of the Bible, we would encourage you to consider other books in the *Knowing the Bible* series, and to visit www.knowingthebibleseries.org.

Lastly, take a moment to look back through this study. Review the notes that you have written and the things that you have highlighted or underlined. Reflect again on the key themes that the Lord has been teaching you about himself and his Word. We pray that these truths and lessons will become a treasure for the rest of your life, in the name of the Father, and the Son, and the Holy Spirit. Amen.